LIFE WITH FATHER

Clarence Day

With acknowledgments to the Editors of *The New Yorker, Harper's Magazine* and *The New Republic,* in which periodicals these chapters first appeared.

CONTENTS

FOREWORD

The affectionate humor and civilized composure that distinguish *Life with Father* are hard to reconcile with what even cursory research into the writer's life reveals: for most of his adult life, Clarence Day suffered from a form of arthritis so debilitating it dictated his daily routine. After graduating from Yale in the class of 1896, he had returned to New York and taken a position in the Wall Street office of the family firm; but by 1903 his physical condition had so deteriorated that he retired from business and transferred his seat on the stock exchange to one of his brothers. From then on, writing and drawing became his main occupations.

"One good thing about rheumatism," he wrote with typical equanimity, "is that it lives in your arms and legs, mainly; in other words, it's mostly the outlying districts that are affected, it doesn't get where you live; so you don't have to think of it much. It doesn't give you the headaches dyspepsia would, or sour your character so, or your views of the world." As we read in the *Dictionary of American Biography,* much of the author's day was devoted to the regimen his condition required, and he seldom began work till evening, often working on his writing through the small hours of the night. "He was ingenious in devising means of overcoming his crippleness," the *Dictionary* informs us, "and when his hands became swollen—into the size of baseball mitts, as he described them—he arranged a pulley to hold up his right hand while he worked."

If it's hard to imagine that Mr. Day junior didn't "have to think of it much," it's harder still to imagine Mr. Day senior—the Father whose demanding personality is so winningly memorialized in the book you hold—suffering such an affliction without rattling the rafters with continuous shouts, oaths, and imperious demands. Indeed, the elder Day's ongoing argument with the order (or lack of order) of things is well characterized in his sickbed imprecation of a higher power, as recorded by his son in "Father is Firm with His Ailments": "'Have mercy,' they heard him shouting indignantly. 'I say have mercy, damn it.'" And just as tellingly in this exchange, from the final chapter of *Life with Father:*

> "Everybody has blood pressure, Mr. Day," the nurse said.
> "A lot of them have," Father replied, "but I haven't. I won't."

Fortunately for him (and especially for his nearest and dearest), Father never had to suffer anything like the painful indignities of his son's illness. Indeed, Father seemed to find the indignities posed by prosperous living painful enough, and most of *Life with Father's* enduring comedy is generated by his large reactions to the small obstacles fate—and his family—put in the way of his pursuit of the standards of pleasure a man of his station might desire to uphold. Given the explosive scale of Father's reaction to everyday vexations, we can safely say it's a good thing he didn't have any blood pressure! Despite Father's continual displays of tyrannical impatience and stubbornness, and his always clueless obduracy as to the effects of his behavior ("I like plenty of ice," Father purrs contentedly as the coda to the commotion of hilarity his determined search for it unleashes in "Father Wakes Up the Village"), the younger Day never seems put out by the older man's actions, never describes him with less than affectionate amusement. Can we take the author's generosity as a tribute to the graciousness of his upbringing in the brownstone New York City of the 1880s and 90s, or as an understanding that the occasional despotism of the paragon of Victorian decorum he loved was merely a reaction against the helter-skelter, yet nonetheless unrelenting, march of modernity? Whatever the motivation for the son's magnanimity, we're glad he takes his Father's antics with such good humor, and that the mythic aura his parent casts holds none of the shadows Dr. Freud would soon discover within the family circle.

While the younger Day enjoyed success throughout his career, producing volumes such as *This Simian World*, in which wit was matched to biting intellect, and becoming one of the early, tone-setting contributors to *The New Yorker*, the reception of *Life with Father* brought his popularity to an entirely new level. Soon after its publication in mid-1935, it was selling one thousand copies a day, and it remained an enduring bestseller, helped no doubt by the theatrical adaptation by Howard Lindsay and Russell Crouse, which opened in 1939 and became one of the longest-lived hits in Broadway history, running for 3,224 performances.

Sadly, the author did not live to see Father dominate the stage, nor even to savor for very long the bestselling status of his book. Clarence Day died in December 1935 at the age of sixty-one, just five months after the publication of *Life with Father*, which, happily, is still with us in all its comic and delightful glory.

James Mustich, Jr.
September 2004

CHAPTER 1

A HOLIDAY WITH FATHER

ONCE IN a long while, as a great treat, Father took me down to his office. This could happen only on a Saturday morning, when there was no school. I felt very important and grown-up on the days I went to "The Office"—not after I got there, to be sure, but as I was leaving the house, with Mother and my three little brothers respectfully seeing me off.

If it was a rainy day, Father would prepare for rough weather by wearing a derby hat and a black rubber mackintosh over his usual tailed coat. (He seldom was informal enough to wear a sack suit in town except on warm days, or when he left New York to go to the country, in summer.) If the sun was out, he wore a silk hat and carried a cane, like his friends. When he and they passed each other on the street, they raised their canes and touched the brims of their hats with them, in formal salute.

I admired this rich and splendid gesture, and wished I could imitate it, but I was too young for a cane. I was soberly dressed in a pepper-and-salt sack suit with short pants and the usual broad flat white Eton collar that boys wore in the eighties—a collar that started out very stiff and immaculate every morning and was done for by

1

dinner time. Black laced or buttoned shoes and black stockings. We only wore brown in the country in summer.

On one of these Saturdays, although it was sunny, Father put on his derby. I didn't know why until later. I hopped along by his side as he walked through the long rows of comfortable-looking brownstone houses from Madison Avenue over to Sixth, climbed the stairs of the Elevated, and stood on the platform, chatting with one of his friends, while we waited for the next train.

Soon a stubby little steam engine, with its open coal car piled full of anthracite, and its three or four passenger cars swinging along behind, appeared round the curve. White smoke poured from the smokestack. The engineer leaned out from his window. "Too-oot, too-too-toot!" whistled the engine as it came puffing in. We got on board and walked leisurely through the cars till Father found a seat that he liked.

During the journey downtown, except when the smoke from the engine was too thick for me to see out, I stared fascinatedly into the windows of cheap red brick tenements, or at the even more interesting interiors of lodging houses for tramps. The second-floor rooms of the lodging houses were crowded, but I envied the tramps in them. They looked so easy-going. Not a thing to do; just tilt their chairs back against the wall, in comfortable old clothes, and smoke. If I were a tramp, I wouldn't have to scrub every last bit of grime out of my knuckles each Friday, and put on tight white kid gloves, and pull some unwieldy little girl around a waxed floor at dancing school. It wouldn't cost so very much, either. The lodging-house sign said in big letters, "Ten Cents a Night."

I never had a chance to see such sights except when I went downtown with Father, for Mother kept away from the Elevated. It was comparatively new, and she felt that the horsecars were better. Besides, Sixth Avenue was so cindery and sooty that ladies disliked it. They did go that far west sometimes, to shop, and they went as far east as Lexington, but in general they lived and walked in the long narrow strip between those two boundaries.

When Father and I left the train at the end of our journey, I found myself in a tangle of little streets full of men and boys but no women. If some lonely bonnet chanced to be bobbing along in the crowd, we all stared at it. Most of the business buildings were old and many of them were dirty, with steep, well-worn wooden stairways, and dark, busy basements. Exchange Place and Broad Street were full of these warrens, and there were some even on Wall Street. The southern corner of Wall Street and Broadway was one of the dingiest. Father raised his cane and said as we passed, "That's where Great-Aunt Lavinia was born."

A few doors beyond the Assay Office we came to a neat but narrow five-story building and walked up the front stoop. This was No. 38 Wall Street. Father's office occupied the ground floor, at the top of the stoop, and on the back part of the second floor he had a small storeroom.

The office was busy in what seemed to me a mysterious way. The cashier, who never would let me go inside his cage, sat in there on a stool, with a cash drawer, a safe full of books, another safe for securities, and a tin box full of postage stamps, which he doled out as needed. One or two bookkeepers were making beautifully written entries in enormous leather-bound ledgers. They had taken the stiff white detachable cuffs off their shirtsleeves and stacked them in a corner, and they had exchanged their regular jackets for black alpaca coats. Future bookkeepers or brokers who now were little office boys ran in and out. Western Union messengers rushed in with telegrams. In the front room there was a long table full of the printed reports issued by railroads about their earnings and traffic. Only twenty or thirty industrial stocks were traded in on the Exchange in those days, and Father's office ignored them. On or around the table were the *Commercial & Financial Chronicle*, the *Journal of Commerce*, a blackboard, a ticker, and four or five whiskery men. Two were arguing heatedly about Henry Ward Beecher, and the others were shaking their heads over some crazy proposal by the "Knights of Labor" to have an eight-hour day.

Father went into his private office, where a little coal fire was burning, hung his hat on a rack, and unlocked and sat down at his desk. While he opened his mail, I proudly brought in two stone jugs of ink, one of greenish black made in England, and one to use when he wrote letters of which he wished to keep copies, because with this ink impressions could be taken to put in his files. I cleaned and filled all Father's inkwells, and put fresh steel pens in his penholders. He had quill pens at home, but he used only steel pens at the office, and as he had no stenographer he wrote a good share of the firm's letters in longhand, himself.

There were lots of things to do in the office besides filling inkwells. It was fun to scamper around the streets carrying all the messages (which are telephoned nowadays), or to roll colored pencils down the clerks' slanting desks, or try to ring the bell on the typewriter. The latter was a new contraption which seldom was used except on important occasions, when the bookkeeper or one of the office boys had to stop work and pick at it.

All of a sudden it was noon. The customers left. The ticker came to a stop. At half past twelve Father called to me and we went out for lunch.

"Will you be back, Mr. Day?" the cashier asked respectfully, but eagerly too. On days when Father said yes, all the clerks looked disappointed. They bent over their desks, saying nothing, till Father went out of the door, but if I lingered behind for a moment I heard them slamming their ledgers about. Not only did they and the office boys all have to stay, but the rule was that they couldn't even smoke until Father had gone home for the day.

Today he said no, however. I saw them getting out their sulphur matches as he was crossing the threshold, and the instant he stepped into the hall they struck them on the seats of their pants.

I trotted along at Father's side down to Beaver Street, where there stood a mellow old building. It had the look of a friendly, hospitable country hotel. There were green blinds and little outside balconies on its upper floors, and windows with looped lacy curtains; and white pillars stood at the entrance, at the top of a low flight of steps.

This was Delmonico's, and the food was so good there that even I had heard it talked of, uptown. It was one of the places that just suited people like Father.

Delmonico's stood upon a triangular-shaped plot of ground, with the front doors at the apex, and when we arrived we met a bottle-necked jam at the entrance. Silk-hatted men, who had been lunching in a lingering way, had suddenly remembered apparently that they were due back in Wall Street, and they were shoving each other, politely but urgently, to force their way out.

As Father and I went in the long crowded room, the head waiter led us with a flourish to a table for two. The air was fragrant with cigar smoke and the appetizing smell of rich, greasy cooking. A stately-looking foreigner who was standing at the side of the room caught Father's eye and bowed to him in a dignified way.

"Lorenzo," Father said to him, as he approached us, "this is my son."

I bobbed my head at him, rather embarrassed, and Mr. Lorenzo Crist Delmonico bowed and said he was happy to meet me.

As he left us, old François, Father's regular waiter, hurried up to our table, and he and Father had a talk, in French, about the best dish to order. They spoke so rapidly that I couldn't understand a word of it, except that François kept assuring Father that we could rely on the sauce. *"Parfaitement."* It seemed that the last time that Father had relied on this sauce, an admittedly difficult kind, he had had a severe disappointment.

When anything of this sort occurred, I had noted, François had a healing way of dealing with such a catastrophe. He seemed even more shocked and perturbed at a failure than Father, and he would snatch the offending dish away and come racing back with a sub- stitute. Usually he was accompanied at such moments by one of the Delmonico family—Lorenzo or Charles—who bent over the table to examine the new dish as it was placed before Father, murmuring most sympathetically about the unhappy misfortune.

Today the sauce and everything else was not only successful but perfect, and Father and François smiled and nodded in a congratulatory way to each other. I used to wonder why Father never got into rages at Delmonico's as he did at home, but I see now that he may have felt lonely at home, where there were no brother experts.

Father was fond of French cooking and of being served by French waiters. At home he had to put up with an Irish waitress who was changed every few months, and with cooking which, though excellent of its kind, after all wasn't French. He ate it with relish and gusto, when it came up to his standards, but he did so like a city man in the country, enjoying good, simple fare.

I didn't always appreciate French cooking myself. It tasted all right, but it was dainty and there wasn't much of it. It seemed to me that Father got along with a very light lunch. When he was having his demi-tasse, however, and saw a hungry look on my face, he smiled understandingly and beckoned to François, who smiled too and presently came running back with a large chocolate éclair. The richness of its soft, thick yellow interior and the meltingness of its chocolate outside were so delicious that time stood still as I happily ate it, and I almost forgot where I was.

After lunch, instead of taking me back uptown, Father walked down to the Battery, and to my surprise we got on the boat at South Ferry. We had never done this before. I now saw why he was wearing his derby. We were going out to the country. Off we steamed across the sweet-smelling bay filled with sail-boats and four-masted schooners and tug-boats and barges, and when we landed on Staten Island Father told me that we were going to see Buffalo Bill.

We got seats in a flimsy wooden stand full of splintery benches, and there was the Wild West spread out before us—dust, horses, and all. The wonderful marksmanship of riders who hit glass balls with their rifles—balls tossed into the air and shot at with careless ease as the horsemen dashed by; the herds of cattle, the lariats, the brass band, the old Deadwood Stage Coach, the thrilling attack on it by Indians, the last-minute rescue. Father dragged me out just before the rescue so that we could get seats on the ferryboat, but I caught a glimpse of it anyway as I was being hauled through the exit.

I wanted to be a cowboy, I told Father on the way home. He chuckled and said no I didn't. He said I might as well be a tramp.

I wondered if I'd better tell him that this idea, too, had occurred to me, no further back than that very morning. I decided that upon the whole it mightn't be a good day to mention it, just after Father had taken me to lunch at Delmonico's. I did venture to ask him, however, what was the matter with cowboys.

Father briefly explained that their lives, their food, and their sleeping accommodations were outlandish and "slummy." They lived in the wilds, he informed me, and they had practically gone wild themselves. "Put your cap on straight," he added. "I am trying to bring you up to be a civilized man."

I adjusted my cap and walked on, thinking over this future. The more I thought about it, the less I wanted to be a civilized man. After all, I had had a very light lunch, and I was tired and hungry. What with fingernails and improving books and dancing school, and sermons on Sundays, the few chocolate éclairs that a civilized man got to eat were not worth it.

CHAPTER 2

FATHER ON HORSEBACK

FATHER HAD been putting on weight and he didn't like it. He was a solidly-built man, but trim and erect, with a light easy step, and his extra pounds made him uncomfortable. He disapproved of them too. When the fat of fat men seemed to come natural to them, Father took it as a good joke; but he felt that it was slovenly to be careless about getting stout.

He talked about this at his club. What the saloon was to poor men and what coffee houses had once been to Londoners, his club was to Father. It was the front and center of his social life. He stopped there for half an hour or so on his way home from the office, or he walked down there at nine in the evening when Mother had gone up to bed. He played a game or two of billiards—not cards—or he had a whisky and soda with Commodore Brown, or he met and sized up distinguished foreigners, whom he usually didn't think much of. Or he sought for advice about fat.

Some members recommended long walks, but Father had always done a good deal of walking. The opinion of the club was that in that case he had better take up riding horseback.

The only proper way to ride horseback, Father felt, was to join one more club. He joined the Riding Club, in East Fifty-eighth Street, which provided stabling and other conveniences, and after practicing in there in the tanbark ring, he rode out in the Park.

The Park itself was only a ring on a larger scale, nothing wild or adventurous; but it suited Father. He disliked wildness—he preferred things like landscapes to be orderly, and suitably arranged for his use. From this time on, he was as critical of the Park as he was of his home. He felt personally affronted for instance when the bridle path wasn't raked properly, or when papers were left lying about.

His first horse was a powerful bay by the name of Rob Roy. This horse didn't like Father, and Father had still less affection for him. This was supposed to be of no importance—it was not even considered. Father bought him because he was spirited and sound, and able to stand work; handsome too. He paid three hundred dollars for him, and expected him to do what he was told.

Rob Roy never looked upon the transaction in this way, however. He had an independent and self-absorbed nature; he was always thinking of his own point of view. Even if he had been devoted to Father, which he never was, this would have made trouble.

One typical scene between them, I remember, occurred near the Park entrance. It was a warm autumn morning. Rob Roy and Father had trotted out of the club and into the Park, each thoroughly healthy and strong, and each intent on his thoughts. They made a fine sight as they went up the bridle path. All their plans coincided. But then a difference between them arose. Father wished to keep on. Rob Roy didn't. I don't know why Rob Roy wanted to stop; perhaps he didn't like the way Father rode him. Anyhow he came to a halt. Father gave him a cut with his whip. Rob Roy whirled around. Father reined him up sharply and struck him again. Rob Roy reared.

As they fought, Father in his anger kept hitting Rob Roy; and Rob Roy violently pawed the ground, and stamped on it, and tore it all up. They both perspired so freely that between them they must have lost gallons, and they both blindly stuck to their respective plans and would not give in.

But Rob Roy had the whole day before him, and Father did not—he had to get through his ride sometime and go to his office. He decided that Rob Roy was crazy, and they returned to the club. Rob Roy was led off to his stall and rubbed down by a groom, and Father went to the dressing-room for members and was rubbed dry by Jim, the attendant.

Jim was a friendly old soul. "Have a nice ride, Mr. Day?" he asked.

"Nice hell," Father shortly replied, and took his cane and went out.

These fierce morning combats gave our family a feeling of awe. We had never dreamed that anyone, man or beast, would resist Father's will. This rashness of Rob Roy's was like Satan's rebelling against God—it had a dark splendor about it, but it somehow filled me with horror.

In that fight between Satan and God, we had been told that God won. There were stray bits of evidence to the contrary lying around, but naturally we had accepted the official announcement. In the long war between Father and Rob Roy, we always assumed Father won, but there too I now see that Rob Roy may have looked at it differently. For the way that Father defeated Rob Roy was by deciding to sell him.

To us boys this seemed like a banishment. It made Rob Roy an outcast. Perhaps it only meant to him meeting a rider less uncongenial; but to us it seemed like obliterating him from the world, in the prime of his life. For years afterward he was spoken of as a strange being, a queer, insane creature, who had unaccountably and vainly attempted to disobey Father.

Rob Roy was a thorough-bred. His successor, a lanky brown horse named Brownie, was plain middle-class. Rob Roy was an adventurer. Brownie was a sad-eyed philosopher. Some philosophers are as great-hearted as adventurers, but they are mostly more docile.

Brownie trotted wherever Father told him to, in any direction. He never once reared, never stamped on the ground, never snorted. There were sometimes little differences of opinion between him and Father, because Brownie got tired sooner than Father did, and wanted to rest. But he never made a direct issue of it, never fought for his rights; he tried to get them either by malingering or by passive resistance. For instance, Father would set out with the plan in his mind of having a glorious gallop, up hill and down dale. Well, Brownie, who had to do the galloping, would keep it up for a while—would keep it up far longer at times than he had ever intended; for he found that a whip kept landing on his flank whenever he started to slacken. But, as he lost heart in the expedition, he also lost spring; and finally he would thump along so heavily that Father let up.

In general however the two got along very well. Father became enthusiastic about the pleasure of riding. Being a hearty, expansive man, he talked of this often, at home. He talked of it so much, in fact, that Mother began to feel he was selfish, in that he was keeping a pleasure for himself which should be shared with his family. If riding around the Park was so exhilarating, she said we all ought to do it.

Father said he wished that we could, but there was only one horse.

This silenced the family for a while; but soon Mother spoke up: she didn't see why the rest of us couldn't ride the horse when Father was through.

The unreasonableness and impracticability of this idea made Father hot. It showed how little Mother knew about anything, especially horses, he said. He explained that Brownie was already inclined to be sluggish, and that he wouldn't be fresh enough for a man to ride if he did extra work.

Mother said firmly, then Father should get some more horses.

This took him aback. He always meant to do the right thing by us; and he began to fear that his own goodness of heart might now get him in trouble. His feeling was that when he innocently had gone in for riding, himself, he had never contemplated having to spend enough to mount the whole family. He said that if he had foreseen that we all would be wanting to ride through the Park, just because he, a hard-working man, got a little relief in that way, he would have gone without the relief, damn it. He would now. He'd sell out.

Of course he had no intention of doing this. Instead he bought one more horse, a younger and happier one, and then gave us boys poor old Brownie.

CHAPTER 3

FATHER IS FIRM WITH HIS AILMENTS

FATHER GOT annoyed at us when we didn't stay well. He usually stayed well himself and he expected us to be like him, and not faint and slump on his hands and thus add to his burdens.

He was fearless about disease. He despised it. All this talk about germs, he said, was merely newfangled nonsense. He said that when he was a boy there had been no germs that he knew of. Perhaps invisible insects existed, but what of it? He was as healthy as they were. "If any damned germs want to have a try at me," he said, "bring 'em on."

From Father's point of view, Mother didn't know how to handle an ailment. He admired her most of the time and thought there was nobody like her; he often said to us boys, "Your mother is a wonderful woman;" but he always seemed to disapprove of her when she was ill.

Mother went to bed, for instance, at such times. Yet she didn't make noises. Father heard a little gasping moan sometimes, but she didn't want him to hear even that. Consequently he was sure she wasn't suffering. There was nothing to indicate it, he said.

The worse she felt, the less she ever said about it, and the harder it was for him to believe that there was anything really wrong with her. "He says he can't see why I stay in bed so long," she once wrote to me, when I was away, "but this colitis is a mean affair which keeps one perfectly flat. The doctor told him yesterday the meaning of colitis, but he said he 'had never heard of the damned thing, thank God.' He feels very abused that he should be 'so upset by people with queer things the matter with them and doctors all over the place.' " (Mother underlined the word "people.")

Even Mother's colds made him fretful. Whenever she had one, she kept going as long as she could, pottering about her room looking white and tired, with a shawl round her shoulders. But sometimes she had to give up and crawl into her bed.

Father pished and poohed to himself about his, and muttered that it was silly. He said Mother was perfectly healthy. When people thought they were ill, he declared, it didn't mean that there was anything the matter with them, it was merely a sign of weak character. He often told Mother how weak it was to give in to an ailment, but every time he tried to strengthen her character in this respect, he said she seemed to resent it. He never remembered to try except when she could hardly hold her head up. From his point of view, though, that was the very time that she needed his help.

He needed hers, too, or not exactly her help but her company, and he never hesitated to say so. When she was ill, he felt lost.

He usually came up from his office at about five or six. The first thing he did was to look around the house to find Mother. It made his home feel queer and empty to him when she wasn't there.

One night about six o'clock he opened the door of her bedroom. There was no light except for a struggling little fire which flickered and sank in the grate. A smell of witch-hazel was in the air, mixed with spirits of camphor. On the bed, huddled up under an afghan, Mother lay still, in the dark.

"Are you there, Vinnie?" Father said, in a voice even louder than usual because of his not being sure.

Mother moaned, "Go away."

"What?" he asked, in astonishment.

"Go away. Oh, go 'way."

"Damnation!" he said, marching out.

"Clare!"

"What is it?"

"Won't you *ple-e-ease* shut my door again!"

Father ground his teeth and shut it with such a bang that it made Mother jump.

He told himself she had nothing the matter with her. She'd be all right in the morning. He ate a good dinner. Being lonely, he added an extra glass of claret and some toasted crackers and cheese. He had such a long and dull evening that he smoked two extra cigars.

After breakfast the next morning, he went to her bedroom again. The fire was out. Two worn old slippers lay on a chair. The gray daylight was cheerless. Father stood at the foot of Mother's bed, looking disconsolately at her because she wasn't well yet. He had no one to laugh at or quarrel with; his features were lumpy with gloom.

"What is it?" Mother asked in a whisper, opening her weary eyes.

"Nothing," he said loudly. "Nothing."

"Well, for mercy's sake, don't come in here looking like that, Clare," Mother begged.

"What do you mean? Looking like what?"

"Oh, go away!" Mother shrieked. "When people are sick, they like to see a smile or something. I never will get well if you stand there and stare at me that way! And shut my door quietly this time. And let me alone."

Outside her door, when I asked him how Mother was, he said with a chuckle: "She's all right again. She isn't out of bed yet, but she sounds much better this morning."

Father's own experiences in a sick-room had been very few. When he was in his early thirties, he had an attack of gout which lasted three weeks. From that time until he was seventy-four and had pneumonia, he had no other serious illnesses. He said illnesses were mostly imaginary and he didn't believe in them.

He even declared that his pneumonia was imaginary. "It's only some idea of that doctor's," he said. "Nothing the matter with me but a cold." Our regular physician had died, and this new man and two trained nurses had all they could do, at first, to keep Father in bed.

The new doctor had pale-blue eyes, a slight build, and a way of inwardly smiling at the persons he talked to. He had a strong will in crises, and he was one of the ablest physicians in town. Mother had chosen him, however, chiefly because she liked one of his female cousins.

When Father got worse, the doctor kept warning him that it really *was* pneumonia, and that if he wouldn't be tractable, he might not get over it—especially at seventy-four.

Father lay in bed glowering at him and said: "I didn't send for you, sir. You needn't stand there and tell me what you want me to do. I know all about doctors. They think they know a damned lot. But they don't. Give your pills and things to Mrs. Day—she believes in them. That's all I have to say. There's no need to continue this discussion. There's the door, sir. Goodbye."

But somehow the discussion kept on, and much to his surprise Father at last became convinced he was ill. The doctor, leaving him alone in his bedroom to digest the bad news, came out in the hall, anxious and tired, to have a few words with Mother. As they stood outside Father's door whispering quietly, they heard his voice from within. Apparently, now that he knew he was in trouble, his thoughts had turned to his God. "Have mercy!" they heard him shouting indignantly. "I say have mercy, damn it!"

Any sufferings that Father ever had he attributed solely to God. Naturally, he never thought for a moment that God could mean him to suffer. He couldn't imagine God's wishing to punish him either, for his conscience was clear. His explanation seemed to be that God was clumsy, not to say muddle-headed.

However, in spite of God and the doctor, Father got over pneumonia, just as, some forty years before, he had got over his gout. Only, in conquering his gout, he had had the help of a cane and a masseur called Old Lowndes.

While the gout was besieging him, Father sat in a big chair by the fire with his bad foot on a stool, armed with a cane which he kept constantly ready. Not that he used the cane to walk with. When he walked, he hopped around on his other foot, uttering strong howls of fury. But he valued his cane highly, and needed it, too, as a war club. He threatened the whole family with it. When visitors entered the room he brandished it fiercely at them, to keep them away from his toe.

Old Lowndes was allowed to approach nearer than others, but he was warned that if he made any mistakes that cane would come down on his head. Father felt there was no knowing what harm Lowndes might have done if he hadn't shaken his cane at him and made him take care. As it was, owing largely to this useful stick, Father got well.

This experience convinced him that any disease could be conquered by firmness.

When he had a cold, his method of dealing with it was to try to clear it out by main force, either by violently blowing his nose or, still better, by sneezing. Mother didn't like him to sneeze, he did it with such a roar. She said she could feel it half across the room, and she was sure it was catching. Father said this was nonsense. He said his sneezes were healthy. And presently we'd hear a hearty, triumphant blast as he sneezed again.

Aside from colds, which he had very seldom, his only foes were sick headaches. He said headaches only came from eating, however. Hence a man who knew enough to stop eating could always get rid of one that way. It took time to starve it out thoroughly. It might take several hours. But as soon as it was gone, he could eat again and enjoy his cigar.

When one of these headaches started, Father lay down and shut his eyes tight and yelled. The severity of a headache could be judged by the volume of sound he put forth. His idea seemed to be to show the headache that he was just as strong as it was, and stronger. When a headache and he went to bed together, they were a noisy pair.

Father's code required him to be game, I suppose. He never spoke or thought of having a code; he wasn't that sort of person; but he denounced men whose standards were low, as to gameness or anything else. It didn't occur to him to conceal his sufferings, however; when he had any pains, he expressed them as fully as he knew how. His way of being brave was not to keep still but to keep on fighting the headache.

Mother used to beg him to be quiet at night, even if he did have a headache, and not wake up the whole house. He never paid the slightest attention to such a request. When she said, "Please don't groan so much, Clare," he'd look at her in disgust, as though he were a warrior being asked to stifle his battle-cries.

One evening he found Mother worrying because Aunt Emma was ill with some disease that was then epidemic.

"Oh, pooh!" Father said. "Nothing the matter with Emma. You can trust people to get any ailment whatever that's fashionable. They hear of a lot of other people having it, and the first thing you know they get scared and think they have it themselves. Then they go to bed, and send for the doctor. The doctor! All poppycock."

"Well, but Clare dear, if you were in charge of them, what would you do instead?"

"Cheer 'em up, that's the way to cure 'em."

"How would you cheer them up, darling?" Mother asked doubtfully.

"I? I'd tell 'em, *'Bah!'* "

CHAPTER 4

FATHER WAKES UP THE VILLAGE

ONE OF the most disgraceful features of life in the country, Father often declared, was the general inefficiency and slackness of small village tradesmen. He said he had originally supposed that such men were interested in business, and that that was why they had opened their shops and sunk capital in them, but no, they never used them for anything but gossip and sleep. They took no interest in civilized ways. Hadn't heard of them, probably. He said that of course if he were camping out on the veldt or the tundra, he would expect few conveniences in the neighborhood and would do his best to forego them, but why should he be confronted with the wilds twenty miles from New York?

Usually, when Father talked this way, he was thinking of ice. He strongly objected to spending even one day of his life without a glass of cold water beside his plate at every meal. There was never any difficulty about this in our home in the city. A great silver ice-water pitcher stood on the sideboard all day, and when Father was home its outer surface was frosted with cold. When he had gone to the office, the ice was allowed to melt sometimes, and the water got warmish, but never in the evening, or on Sundays, when Father might want some. He said he liked water, he told us it was one of Nature's best gifts, but he said that like all her gifts it was unfit for human consumption unless served in a suitable manner. And the only right way to serve water was icy cold.

It was still more important that each kind of wine should be served at whatever the right temperature was for it. And kept at it, too. No civilized man would take dinner without wine, Father said, and no man who knew the first thing about it would keep his wine in hot cellars. Mother thought this was a mere whim of Father's. She said he was fussy. How about people who lived in apartments, she asked him, who didn't have cellars? Father replied that civilized persons didn't live in apartments.

One of the first summers that Father ever spent in the country, he rented a furnished house in Irvington on the Hudson, not far from New York. It had a garden, a stable, and one or two acres of woods, and Father arranged to camp out there with many misgivings. He took a train for New York every morning at eight-ten, after breakfast, and he got back between five and six, bringing anything special we might need along with him, such as a basket of peaches from the city, or a fresh package of his own private coffee.

Things went well until one day in August the ice-man didn't come. It was hot, he and his horses were tired, and he hated to come to us anyhow because the house we had rented was perched up on top of a hill. He said afterward that on this particular day he had not liked the idea of making his horses drag the big ice-wagon up that sharp and steep road to sell us fifty cents' worth of ice. Besides, all his ice was gone anyhow—the heat had melted it on him. He had four or five other good reasons. So he didn't come.

Father was in town. The rest of us waited in astonishment, wondering what could be the matter. We were so used to the regularity and punctilio of life in the city that it seemed unbelievable to us that the ice-man would fail to appear. We discussed it at lunch. Mother said that the minute he arrived she would have to give him a talking to. After lunch had been over an hour and he still hadn't come, she got so worried about what Father would say that she decided to send to the village.

There was no telephone, of course. There were no motors. She would have liked to spare the horse if she could, for he had been worked hard that week. But as this was a crisis, she sent for Morgan, the coachman, and told him to bring up the dog-cart.

The big English dog-cart arrived. Two of us boys and the coachman drove off. The sun beat down on our heads. Where the heavy harness was rubbing on Brownie's coat, he broke out into a thick, whitish lather. Morgan was sullen. When we boys were along he couldn't take off his stiff black high hat or unbutton his thick, padded coat. Worse still, from his point of view, he couldn't stop at a bar for a drink. That was why Mother had sent us along with him, of course, and he knew it.

We arrived at the little town after a while and I went into the Coal & Ice Office. A wiry-looking old clerk was dozing in a corner, his chair tilted back and his chin resting on his dingy shirt-front. I woke this clerk up. I told him about the crisis at our house.

He listened unwillingly, and when I had finished he said it was a very hot day.

I waited. He spat. He said he didn't see what he could do, because the ice-house was locked.

I explained earnestly that this was the Day family and that something must be done right away.

He hunted around his desk a few minutes, found his chewing tobacco, and said, "Well, sonny, I'll see what I can do about it."

I thanked him very much, as that seemed to me to settle the matter. I went back to the dog-cart. Brownie's check-rein had been unhooked, and he stood with his head hanging down. He looked sloppy. It wouldn't have been so bad with a buggy, but a slumpy horse in a dog-cart can look pretty awful. Also, Morgan was gone. He reappeared soon, coming out of a side door down the street, buttoning up his coat, but with his hat tilted back. He looked worse that the horse.

We checked up the weary animal's head again and drove slowly home. A hot little breeze in our rear moved our dust along with us. At the foot of the hill, we boys got out, to spare Brownie our extra weight. We unhooked his check-rein again. He dragged the heavy cart up.

Mother was sitting out on the piazza. I said the ice would come soon now. We waited.

It was a long afternoon.

At five o'clock, Brownie was hitched up again. The coachman and I drove back to the village. We had to meet Father's train. We also had to break the bad news to him that he would have no ice-water for dinner, and that there didn't seem to be any way to chill his Rhine wine.

The village was as sleepy as ever, but when Father arrived and learned what the situation was, he said it would have to wake up. He told me that he had had a long, trying day at the office, the city was hotter than the Desert of Sahara, and he was completely worn out, but that if any ice-man imagined for a moment he could behave in that manner, he, Father, would take his damned head off. He strode into the Coal & Ice Office.

When he came out, he had the clerk with him, and the clerk had put on his hat and was vainly trying to calm Father down. He was promising that he himself would come with the ice-wagon if the driver had left, and deliver all the ice we could use, and he'd be there inside an hour.

Father said, "Inside of an hour be hanged, you'll have to come quicker than that."

The clerk got rebellious. He pointed out that he'd have to go to the stables and hitch up the horses himself, and then get someone to help him hoist a block of ice out of the ice-house. He said it was 'most time for his supper and he wasn't used to such work. He was only doing it as a favor to Father. He was just being neighborly.

Father said he'd have to be neighborly in a hurry, because he wouldn't stand it, and he didn't know what the devil the ice company meant by such actions.

The clerk said it wasn't his fault, was it? It was the driver's.

This was poor tactics, of course, because it wound Father up again. He wasn't interested in whose fault it was, he said. It was everybody's. What he wanted was ice and plenty of it, and he wanted it in time for his dinner. A small crowd which had collected by this time listened admiringly as Father shook his finger at the clerk and said he dined at six-thirty.

The clerk went loping off toward the stables to hitch up the big horses. Father waited till he'd turned the corner.

Followed by the crowd, Father marched to the butcher's.

After nearly a quarter of an hour, the butcher and his assistant came out, unwillingly carrying what seemed to be a coffin, wrapped in a black mackintosh. It was a huge cake of ice.

Father got in, in front, sat on the box seat beside me, and took up the reins. We drove off. The coachman was on the rear seat, sitting back-to-back to us, keeping the ice from sliding out with the calves of his legs. Father went a few doors up the street to a little house-furnishings shop and got out again.

I went in the shop with him this time. I didn't want to miss any further scenes of this performance. Father began proceedings by demanding to see all the man's ice-boxes. There were only a few. Father selected the largest he had. Then, when the sale seemed arranged, and when the proprietor was smiling broadly with pleasure at this sudden windfall, Father said he was buying that refrigerator only on two conditions.

The first was that it had to be delivered at his home before dinner. Yes, now. Right away. The shopkeeper explained over and over that this was impossible, but that he'd have it up the next morning, sure. Father said no, he didn't want it the next morning, he had to have it at once. He added that he dined at six-thirty, and that there was no time to waste.

The shopkeeper gave in.

The second condition, which was then put to him firmly, was staggering. Father announced that that ice-box must be delivered to him full of ice.

The man said he was not in the ice business.

Father said, "Very well then. I don't want it."

The man said obstinately that it was an excellent ice-box.

Father made a short speech. It was the one that we had heard so often at home about the slackness of village tradesmen, and he put such strong emotion and scorn in it that his voice rang through the shop. He closed it by saying, "An ice-box is of no use to a man without ice, and if you haven't the enterprise, the gumption, to sell your damned goods to a customer who wants them delivered in condition to use, you had better shut up your shop and be done with it. Not in the ice business, hey? You aren't in business at all!" He strode out.

The dealer came to the door just as Father was getting into the dog-cart, and called out anxiously, "All right, Mr. Day. I'll get the refrigerator filled for you and sent it up right away."

Father drove quickly home. A thunderstorm seemed to be brewing and this had waked Brownie up, or else Father was putting some of his own supply of energy into him. The poor old boy probably needed it as again he climbed the steep hill. I got out at the foot, and as I walked along behind I saw that Morgan was looking kind of desperate, trying to sit in the correct position with his arms folded while he held in the ice with his legs. The big cake was continually slipping and sliding around under the seat and doing its best to plunge out. It had bumped against his calves all the way home. They must have got good and cold.

When the dog-cart drew up at our door, Father remained seated a moment while Morgan, the waitress, and I pulled and pushed at the ice. The mackintosh had come off it by this time. We dumped it out on the grass. A little later, after Morgan had unharnessed and hurriedly rubbed down the horse, he ran back to help us boys break the cake up, push the chunks around to the back door, and cram them into the ice-box while Father was dressing for dinner.

Mother had calmed down by this time. The Rhine wine was cooling. "Don't get it too cold," Father called.

Then the ice-man arrived.

The old clerk was with him, like a warden in charge of a prisoner. Mother stepped out to meet them, and at once gave the ice-man the scolding that had been waiting for him all day.

The clerk asked how much ice we wanted. Mother said we didn't want any now. Mr. Day had brought home some, and we had no room for more in the ice-box.

The ice-man looked at the clerk. The clerk tried to speak, but no words came.

Father put his head out of the window. "Take a hundred pounds, Vinnie," he said. "There's another box coming."

A hundred-pound block was brought into the house and heaved into the washtub. The waitress put the mackintosh over it. The ice-wagon left.

Just as we all sat down to dinner, the new ice-box arrived, full.

Mother was provoked. She said "Really, Clare!" crossly. "Now what am I to do with that piece that's waiting out in the washtub?"

Father chuckled.

She told him he didn't know the first thing about keeping house, and went out to the laundry with the waitress to tackle the problem. The thunderstorm broke and crashed. We boys ran around shutting the windows upstairs.

Father's soul was at peace. He dined well, and he had his coffee and cognac served to him on the piazza. The storm was over by then. Father snuffed a deep breath of the sweet-smelling air and smoked his evening cigar.

"Clarence," he said, "King Solomon had the right idea about these things. 'Whatsoever thy hand findeth to do,' Solomon said, 'do thy damnedest.' "

Mother called me inside. "Whose mackintosh is that?" she asked anxiously. "Katie's torn a hole in the back."

I heard Father saying contentedly on the piazza, "I like plenty of ice."

CHAPTER 5

FATHER DECLINES TO BE KILLED

I DON'T know why Father and Mother chose Irvington to go to, that summer. There were lots of other places where we boys could have enjoyed ourselves better, but we weren't consulted of course, and we'd have been surprised if we had been. The family assumed that we could have a good time anywhere. We had supposed so ourselves. But everything was wrong about Irvington.

I used to sit up on our hill and stare down at the Hudson. It had a dirty yellow-brown color, it didn't make any noises, and I felt I never had seen such a tiresome river. Compared to the blue salt-water we were used to, it seemed too dull and lifeless to swim in. There was no bathing beach anyhow.

Down the road was the old Washington Irving house in Sleepy Hollow, which Mother insisted was lovely, but it was still as death, and two thin little old ladies who mustn't be disturbed sat and rocked on the porch.

About an hour's walk in the other direction there was a fat boy who had rabbits, but we didn't think much of either those rabbits or the fellow who owned them.

On our hill we were surrounded by great, silent, park-like estates, belonging to great, silent, rich men who didn't want boys around. We occasionally explored these parks uninvited, but they weren't any good. And the hill that we lived on was as limited a hill as we'd ever seen.

Our garden seemed to be owned by the gardener. He wouldn't let us go in it. He doled out flowers from it to Mother and he scowled when he brought in the vegetables. When Mother asked him when he'd have more tomatoes or peas, he used to think deeply and say, "She be up in two day." He complained of the large amounts of vegetables the cook said we needed. At the end of the season we found he'd been selling the best of the produce all summer.

On one side of the garden was a small grove of trees, called "the woods." We spent most of our time in a swampy hollow in there, building a house in the underbrush. I was the Pharaoh of this sweaty enterprise and my brothers served as my subject Egyptians, at first. But as time went on and as it began to dawn upon them that this house would be mine when they finished it, they lost interest in it, and I had to do more and more of the work myself. It was a good little house, though. Its chief defect was that it was damp. It had no drainage and the trees kept dripping on it. It almost never felt dry. Also, as there was very little room in it, only one person—not counting the mosquitoes—could get inside at a time. That one person was nearly always me, until I came down with malaria.

When I got out of bed again, wandering around in the old graystone house during my long convalescence, I found thirty or forty yellow paper-bound books in the garret. The only books that Father and Mother didn't like me to read were cheap sensational novels with yellow-paper covers, such as were sold at railroad news-stands. I had always obeyed them till now, but here were a lot of those very books right in the house, and here was I feeling for the first time in my life bored and idle. I took two of the novels downstairs with me and hid them in my bedroom closet.

After that I went to bed early every night and eagerly read those two books, hungry for adventures of any kind, even of love. I was thirteen, and love affairs were beginning to seem faintly interesting. The tedious thing about such affairs to my mind was their sickening flavor of sweetness, but in yellow-backed paper novels I hopefully assumed that they'd be less true-hearted than in other books, and more illicit, more lurid.

To my astonishment I found that this wasn't so. There was nothing sensational in those novels. I read them all the way through to make sure, but I seemed to have drawn two blanks. I took them back up to the garret and brought down some more.

I kept doggedly on through the whole collection, and when I had finished I made up my mind never to read a yellow-backed novel again. Instead of being sinful and gay they were full of moral reflections. They even had clergymen in them. They were all by one man, a writer named Anthony Trollope, whom I never had heard of, and who didn't seem much of a success at sensational fiction. I put them back up in the garret.

I didn't tell my parents about Trollope. He became one of my guilty secrets.

There had been a great deal of talk before we went to the country about what kind of carriage we'd need, for Father to drive to the station in and for Mother to use making calls. We had never owned a carriage before.

There didn't seem to be any such thing as a general-utility vehicle. A two-seated surrey would have been the nearest thing to it, but Father said that a liveried coachman wouldn't look right in a surrey, unless he were driving it, and Father wished to do the driving himself. That ruled out victorias, too. Mother said that next to a victoria she'd choose a nice buggy, but Father said that a buggy would be no use to us when we went back to town. Nobody but a countryman would drive in New York in a buggy. He said he had always loathed buggies, and that he would as lief go around in a wheelbarrow. In the end he had gone to Brewster's to get their advice, and they had fitted him out with that big English dog-cart I spoke of. When Mother remonstrated, he said that Brewster's were the best carriage-builders he knew, and the upshot of it was that Mother was driven around in that dog-cart for years.

It seemed very pleasant to us boys to drive in that dog-cart. It was high, and it had no bothersome doors, sides, or windows, like cabs. On rainy days, the coachman put rubber covers on the cushions and we wore rubber coats. It was a strong heavy vehicle that would stand a lot of knocking about. But it had only two wheels, of course, and it didn't suit Mother. She said it jiggled too much. No matter how tightly she pinned on her hat, Sunday mornings, she arrived at the church door shaken loose on top and bunched up below. And the combination or rain and a dog-cart didn't suit her at all.

The very first drive that we took in it, there was a shower. The dog-cart was stopped. Father and Mother and I and Morgan, the coachman, stood up and put on our rubber coats, and Morgan got out the large rubber apron. Mother then raised her umbrella to protect her big ribbony hat.

Father, sitting on the box seat beside her, stared at this in horror. "You can't put up that thing," he said.

"I can so," Mother answered indignantly.

"I can't drive if you do," Father said. "How the devil can a man see to drive with you bobbing that big thing in front of us?"

"I'm *not* bobbing it," Mother cried. "It's the wind. Do please hurry, Clare. This is awful!"

"Awful?" said Father, trying to hold his whip crosswise, with the umbrella jerking and beating against it. "It's damnable."

"Well then, why didn't you get a buggy, as I told you?" said Mother.

"Will you kindly hold that thing out of my way?" Father shouted. "Upon my soul, this is positively disgraceful. Stop, Vinnie! Stop! You're poking it right in my eye! You can't carry an umbrella in a dog-cart."

When we arrived at the house, half an hour later, with the rain pouring down, they were still hotly debating this question. I don't remember that it ever was settled, though it was debated for years.

One windy night, a week later, there was another and heavier storm, which began just as Father and Cousin Julie were going out to a dinner party. Neither of them wanted to go, and Julie hadn't even been invited, but Mother declared that they had to. She had written and accepted the invitation for Father and herself ten days ago, she explained, and it was only because she really felt too ill to stir that she was sending Julie instead. Father said he felt sick himself, a lot sicker than Mother, but Mother said he couldn't back out at the last moment and there was no time to send word. So she hurried them off in their evening finery in that cold wind and rain, up high in the air on that shelterless dog-cart, along the unlighted roads.

In general, the roads around Irvington were dusty but good. The great trouble was they were hilly. So far as we boys were concerned, we liked them, but Brownie did not. Brownie was not made for hills, and neither, of course, was the dog-cart. Father said it would have been better to have had a short, stocky cob for such work. Brownie was of an opposite type, he was lanky and limp—so limp that Mother said he was becoming unnaturally elongated, pulling that cart up those hills.

On the other hand, it was because of those hills that our horseback rides were such fun. Father rode every morning before he took the train to the city, and we boys took turns going with him. Little by little we explored every inch of that beautiful countryside.

I was riding with Father one day in September when he found a new road. I galloped ahead, up a hill. Just over the crest of it, hidden from sight till it was too late to stop, was a wash-out—a deep, ditchlike chasm across the road—which my horse luckily jumped, almost before I had seen it. A little farther on I reined him in and looked back, to see if Father had cleared it.

Father was lying face downward in the road. His horse, which had fallen beside him, was thrashing around with its feet. It scrambled up just as I turned, and I saw it step over Father.

I galloped back, dismounted, and managed to roll and push Father over. He was senseless. I sat down in the road with his head on my lap and wiped the blood off his face. I had never seen him helpless before. It gave me a strange feeling.

I had slung the reins of the two horses over my arm. They kept pulling and tugging to get at the grass on the bank.

As Father didn't come to, or stir, I began shouting for help. It was a still Sunday morning. The road ran through cornfields and pastures, and there were no passers-by.

Presently, as I sat there, making all the noise I could, I saw Father frown. His eyes were shut; gravel and mud were ground into his face and he looked done for; but I now felt more hope. I threw back my head, and yelled louder than ever. "Hi! Hi! Hi there, help!"

'Way off in a hollow was a yellow farmhouse. At last I saw a man coming out of it. He shut the door and walked down a grassy path and up the hill toward us.

He got Father to his feet, after a while. We went slowly along to the house with Father stumbling between us. We put him in a chair, on the grass, and washed his face. He held his head up better after this, but he didn't seem to understand questions.

The farmer and I anxiously discussed different plans. We decided I'd better unsaddle my horse and hitch up to the farmer's buggy, put Father in, and drive him home just as quick as I could.

Father paid no attention to what we were doing. When the buggy was ready, however, and we tried to pick him up and dump him in, he objected. He was so groggy and his muscles were so slumpy he could hardly sit up, but he clung to the idea that he was out for a nice morning ride. He absolutely refused to have anything to do with a buggy. "Take that damn thing away," he said, and added that he wanted his horse.

The farmer and I were taken aback by this. We had naturally supposed that we were in charge of things, and that Father's ideas didn't count. I still thought so. I told the farmer that all Father needed was a little persuasion. We tried a great deal of it. We got nowhere at all. Shaken up though he was, Father's firm belief in his impregnability remained unimpaired, and he was still somehow the master of the whole situation.

He kept on demanding his horse so imperiously that I gave in. I unharnessed my own horse and resaddled him, put the buggy back in the barn, and with the greatest misgivings the farmer and I hoisted Father up on his mount. He looked as though he'd fall off every minute, but to our amazement he didn't. I said goodbye to the farmer, and Father and I rode up the hill.

It was a long, silent ride. Father came out of his stupor at moments better that I had hoped. At other times he sank back and wobbled about in the saddle. But his knees held on, even when he shut his eyes and seemed not to know what was happening.

We got back to the main road at last. Farther on we came to Dr. Coudert's place. I got off and rang the front doorbell.

Dr. Coudert was upstairs, dressing for church. He looked out of his bedroom window.

"Why, good morning, Day," he called down to Father. "What's the matter?"

"Marrer is," Father said thickly, "some accident. Want you come my house. Fix it."

He turned and trotted away, lurching in the saddle. I hurried off after him.

At our doorway, when he saw Mother come running out, exclaiming at our being late, he tried to dismount by himself. "Vinnie, dear Vinnie," he muttered, and toppled into our arms.

We got him to bed. Dr. Coudert found a great, dull, dark-red place at the nape of his neck, and said that it was pretty serious, but that there was nothing to do but apply icebags and wait.

Mother immediately telegraphed to Uncle Hal. He was Father's elder brother; he had retired from business and he was taking his ease at some summer resort, which he did not wish to leave, but he took a train and got up to Irvington that same afternoon. Mother explained to him that Father had to have somebody run the office for him, and that Uncle Hal was the only one whom he would trust.

Uncle Hal knew Father too well to take this as a compliment. Father trusted him more than others, yes; but, as Uncle Hal knew from long experience, Father didn't like to trust anyone.

However, Uncle Hal began spending his days down in Wall Street, and faithfully coming up to Irvington to make his reports. He was a large, stout, phlegmatic man, with a face that seemed to be carved from old wood, he could make it so completely expressionless. In behind this, if you watched his eye closely, you could sometimes see a twinkle.

One afternoon when I was in Father's room, changing his icebags, Uncle Hal tiptoed heavily in, and sat down at the side of the bed. He told Father about a few routine matters, in his deliberate way, and then put his fingers together and waited to be cross-examined.

Father feverishly began firing questions at him. "What did you do about those Rome Watertown bonds?" he demanded. "Did you straighten out those legal matters with Choate & Larocque?" The answers to these and other questions were only half-satisfactory. Uncle Hal was a thoroughly sound, careful man; he had made no mistakes, and there was nothing that Father could reasonably object to, exactly, but it exasperated him to discover that his office was not being conducted in quite his own regular manner. "I won't have my office run that way!" he finally roared.

Uncle Hal looked at him stolidly.

Mother rushed in. "Oh, Hal, what *are* you doing!" she shrieked. "I begged you not to excite him!"

Uncle Hal turned his large frame half around in his chair and regarded Mother stolidly too.

"Never knew such a damned way of doing things in my life," Father groaned.

"Come, Hal!" Mother cried. "Come out here in the hall with me, and let me explain *again* to you! Don't sit there, Hal, making things worse like this."

They went out together.

Later on, looking out of the window, I saw Uncle Hal slowly heave himself up into the dog-cart, which always shook him up like a jelly, and which he hated like poison. The coachman drove him off, jiggetty-jig, jiggetty-jog, to the station.

It was weeks before Father got up again. I suppose he had had a concussion of the brain, but we boys weren't told any details. All we knew was that Father had to stay in bed and that he was strangely quiet at first, although later he became his old self again and made a great deal of noise about it. Meanwhile I had a fine time riding his horse, which had more spirit than ours.

After Father got well, he seemed to want to forget the whole incident. He never went back to see that farmer who had tried to lend him his buggy. He didn't seem appreciative of what Mother had done either, she felt, until one day, as a surprise, he gratefully bought her a beautiful ring with three rubies. When Dr. Coudert heard about this, he strongly approved. He told Father that he owed his life to Mother, she had been such a good nurse; and when Mother heard him say it, she nodded her head violently and said that was true.

CHAPTER 6

FATHER HIRES A COOK

ONE LATE afternoon when Father came up from downtown, he found his home much upset. Our cook had walked out and left us. I was a child of four, George was two, and there was a new baby besides. Mother was ill. She hadn't been able to leave us to go to an agency. And as she was no hand at cooking herself, the outlook for dinner was poor.

This state of affairs was unprecedented in all Father's experience. In his father's home, they never changed their servants suddenly; they seldom changed them at all; and as his mother was a past mistress of cooking, he had always been doubly protected. Since his marriage, he had had to live a much bumpier life. But his was the worst yet.

He asked Mother, who was lying in bed, what she was going to do about it. There were no telephones then, and she couldn't do anything at all, at the moment; but she said she would try to go to an agency in the morning and see what she could find. "In the morning? Good God!" Father said. "Where is the place, anyhow?" And he clapped on his hat and strode out again, over toward Sixth Avenue.

As I heard the story years afterward, it was late when he got there, and he bounded up the front stoop two or three steps at a time, and went quickly into the little office, where the gaslights were burning. He had never been in such a place before, and to his surprise it was empty, except for a severe-looking woman who sat at a desk at one side. "Where do you keep 'em?" he urgently demanded, his mind on the question of dinner.

She looked at him, got out her pen, and opened a large book deliberately. "I will take your name and address," she informed him, "and then, if you please, you may give me the details as to what kind of person you require and when you would wish her to call."

But Father had no time, he told her, for any damned fol-de-rol. "Where do you keep 'em?" he said again. She was standing in the way of his dinner. I can imagine how his face must have reddened and how his eyes must have blazed at her. "I am asking you where you keep them!" he roared.

"Why, the girls are in there," the lady explained, to calm him, "but clients are not allowed in that room. If you will tell me the kind of position you wish me to fill for you, I will have one come out."

Before she'd half finished, Father had thrown open the door and gone in. There sat a crowd of the girls, young and old, sickly and brawny, of all shapes and sizes; some ugly, some pretty and trim and stylish, some awkward; nurses, ladies' maids, waitresses, washerwomen, and cooks.

The manager was by now at Father's elbow, trying to make him get out, and insisting that he tell her the position he wished her to fill. But Father was swiftly glancing around at the crowd, and he paid no attention. He noticed a little woman in the corner, with honest gray eyes, who sat there, shrewd-looking and quiet. He pointed his cane over at her and said, "I'll take that one."

The manager was flustered, but still she kept trying to enforce her authority. She protested she didn't yet know the position. . . .

"Cook," Father said, "cook."

"But Margaret doesn't wish to be a cook, she wants—"

"You can cook, can't you?" Father demanded.

Margaret's plain little face was still pink with excitement and pleasure at being chosen above all that roomful by such a masterful gentleman. Father had probably smiled at her, too, for they liked each other at once. Well, she said, she had cooked for one family.

"Of course she can cook," Father said.

He said afterward, when describing the incident, "I knew at once she could cook."

The manager didn't like this at all. The discipline of the office was spoiled. "If you are going to take her anyhow," she said acidly, "what day would you wish her to come, and will you please give me your name?"

"Yes, yes," Father said, without giving it. "Come on, Margaret." And he planked down the fee and walked out.

Margaret followed him through the door and trotted over to our home at his heels. He sent her down to the kitchen immediately, while he went upstairs to dress.

"I don't know why you make such a fuss about engaging new servants. It's simple enough," he said comfortably to Mother that evening, after Margaret's first dinner.

It was the first of a long series, for she stayed with us twenty-six years.

CHAPTER 7

FATHER FEELS STARVED

IN THE summers, when we went to the country, our usual plan was to hire a temporary cook to go with us, so that Margaret could stay in town. We hated to leave her, but the idea was that somebody must stay to take care of the house. There were no electric burglar alarms in those days, and few special watchmen. Little Margaret made a pretty small watchman, for she was no size at all, but she had an indomitable spirit. So we'd leave her on guard while we went up to our summer home in Harrison with a substitute cook.

But this didn't work well. No matter how few the substitute's faults were, Father had no patience with them. One summer, I remember, there was a nice woman, Delia, who got on well with Mother because she was so obliging and pleasant, but who didn't suit Father at all. "I don't give a damn how obliging she is," he kept saying. "If she won't oblige me by cooking something fit to eat, she can go."

This didn't sound unreasonable, but Delia cooked well enough for the rest of us, and Mother hated to risk getting someone else who'd be temperamental. Our dining-room consequently became a battleground morning and night. At breakfast, Father would put down his coffee cup in disgust and roar: "Slops! Damn it, slops! Does she call this confounded mess coffee? Isn't there a damned soul in Westchester County who knows how to make coffee but me? I swear to God I can't even imagine how she concocts such atrocities. I come down to this room hungry every morning, and she tries to fill me with slops! Take it away, I tell you!" he would bellow to the waitress. "Take this accursed mess away!" And while she and Delia were frantically hurrying to make a fresh pot, he would savagely devour his omelet and bacon, and declare that his breakfast was ruined.

The longer Delia stayed with us, the more alarmed Father became. He ate heartily, as Mother kept pointing out to him, but he said he didn't feel nourished. He said it was no use to argue about it; he felt all gone inside. One night after he had had a four-course dinner, he fretfully got up from the table, went into the library with his cigar, and moaned that he was starved. His moans were, as always, full-throated, and they came from the heart. Every now and then, when his miserable condition seemed to strike him afresh, he laid down his book and shouted "Starved! Starved!" in a grief-stricken roar.

When Mother went in the library to quiet him, he told her he'd be damned if he'd stand it. "I refuse to be sent to my grave, do you hear me, by that infernal bog-trotting imbecile you keep in my kitchen."

"Now Clare, a Japanese is coming tomorrow, I told you. This is Delia's last night. I do hope you'll like Tobo. He won't know our ways right at the start, of course, but he is a very good cook."

Father was appeased for the moment by the dismissal of Delia. But the next night, when he found that the first dish was too Oriental, he said in an annoyed tone to Mother, "Will you kindly explain to your man Tobo that I am not a coolie?" And after eating the rest of his dinner, he pushed his plate away and went up to his bedroom, declaring vehemently that he was poisoned. He undressed, lay down on his sofa, and filled the air with deep groans.

From time to time he stopped and dozed a little, or listened to what he could hear of our talk. His feeling was that we shouldn't be talking at all. We ought to be sitting with bowed heads in silence until he recovered. "Poisoned!" he suddenly boomed, to remind us. "Oh, God! I am poisoned!"

At this point, Mother, who was down in the library, laughed. Father heard her. He jumped up from his sofa and marched from his bedroom indignantly into the hall. "I'm a sick man!" he thundered robustly. "And nobody in this house gives a damn!"

Mother hurried upstairs to see what he wanted. He insisted on her rubbing his back. Sick or well, that always soothed him, and he would have liked her to do it for hours. He loved to close his eyes, with someone's hand moving quietly on him, while a feeling of comfort flowed into his thoughts and his nerves.

Mother didn't think much of rubbing, however. She didn't like it herself. When anyone rubbed her, she stiffened and resisted at once. Consequently she had no idea of the right way to do it. When she had to rub Father, she always got tired of it in a very few minutes.

She gave him some hasty little rubs and digs as well as she could, but just as he was beginning to relax, she said, "There now, Clare, that's enough." Father was so disappointed by this that it reminded him that he was poisoned, and the only cure he could think of was the dismissal of Tobo.

The next day old Margaret was sent for to come at once to the country, and the house in town was locked up and left to take care of itself.

She came in a hack from the Harrison station. She was an odd sight. Her face looked familiar in her little black bonnet, tied under her chin, but she seemed strangely swollen and bulky; she stuck out in queer places; and as she crowded through the back door, she bruised me with her hard, bony hip. Only it wasn't her hip, it turned out; it was her favorite saucepan, which was tied to her waist under her skirt. Several large spoons, a dipper, a skillet, and two pair of shoes were made fast under it elsewhere. In her arms she had some bundles wrapped in newspapers, which Mother thought at first held her clothes, but when Margaret opened them we found they contained cheeses, melons, fresh coffee, a leg of lamb, some sweet potatoes, and other provisions. Margaret had no faith at all in being able to buy any supplies in the country. She had brought as complete a larder to Harrison as though we were at the North Pole.

"But didn't you bring any clothes with you, Margaret? Not even an apron?" asked Mother.

Little Margaret pursed her lips closely together and didn't answer at first. Then, as Mother stood waiting, she said unwillingly, "I have me other clothes on me."

She had wanted to have her hands free, it seemed, to bring us something good to eat. So under her street dress she was wearing two other dresses on that hot summer day, a collection of stiffly starched petticoats, three aprons, two nightgowns, and pretty much all the rest of her wardrobe.

As she was climbing upstairs to unpeel and unpack herself, Father saw her. "Is that you, Margaret?" he called, suddenly feeling much better. "Thank God!"

CHAPTER 8

FATHER THUMPS ON THE FLOOR

OLD MARGARET was just the kind of cook that we wanted. Lots of cooks can do rich dishes well. Margaret couldn't. But she cooked simple, everyday dishes in a way that made our mouths water. Her apple pies were the most satisfying pies I've ever tasted. Her warmed-up potatoes were so delicious I could have made my whole dinner of them.

Yet even Margaret sometimes miscalculated. A large, royal-looking steak would be set before Father, which, upon being cut into, would turn out to be too underdone. Father's face would darken with disappointment. If the earth had begun to wobble and reel in its orbit he could scarcely have been more disapproving. He would raise his foot, under the table, and stamp slowly and heavily three times on the rug. Thud; thud; thud.

At this solemn signal, we would hear Margaret leave the kitchen below us and come clumping step by step up the stairs to the dining-room door.

"Margaret, look at that steak."

Margaret would step nearer and peer with a shocked look at the
platter. "The Lord bless us and save us," she would say to herself in
a low voice. She would then seize the platter and make off with it,
to better it the best way she could, and Father would gloomily wait
and eat a few vegetables and pour out a fresh glass of claret.

Father and Margaret were united by the intense interest they
both took in cooking. Each understood the other instinctively. They
had a complete fellow-feeling. Mother's great interest was in babies—
she had never been taught how to cook. All she wanted was to keep
Father pleased somehow; and if it was too difficult she didn't always
care about even that.

At table it was Father who carved the fowl, or sliced the roast lamb
or beef. I liked to watch him whet the knife and go at it. He had such
a fine, easy hand. To a hungry boy, he seemed over-deliberate and
exact in his strokes, yet in a moment or two he had done. And usually the cooking had been as superb as the carving. Sometimes it was
so perfect that Father's face would crinkle with pleasure, and with a
wink at us he'd summon Margaret with his usual three measured
thumps. She would appear, clutching her skirts with both hands, and
looking worried. "What's wanting?" she'd ask.

"Margaret," Father would tell her affectionately, "that fricasseed
chicken is *good.*"

Margaret would turn her wrinkled face aside, and look down, and
push the flat of her hand out toward Father. It was the same gesture
she used when she said "Get along with you" to flatterers. She couldn't
say that to Father, but she would beam at him, and turn and go out,
and stump back down the dark little stairs without ever a word.

Every once in a while, when the household bills were getting too
high, a platter with three tiny French chops on it would be placed
before Father, and a larger dish full of cold corned beef or Irish stew
before Mother. At this sight we boys would stop talking and become
round-eyed and still.

Father would look over at Mother's dish to see if it seemed appetizing, for he often said there was nothing better than one of Margaret's

stews. The stew usually seemed possible enough to him, yet not quite what he wanted. He would then ask Mother if she'd have a chop.

Mother always said, "No."

"They look nice and juicy," Father would urge her, but she would say again she didn't want any, and turn her eyes away from the platter.

Father would then look around at the rest of us, doubtfully. He had four sons, all with appetites. He would clear his throat as though getting ready to offer a chop to each boy in turn; but he usually compromised by saying, "Will anyone else have a chop?"

"No, Clare," Mother would quickly and impatiently reply, "they're for you. The rest of us are going to have stew tonight." And she'd smile brightly but a little watchfully around at us boys, to be sure that we were making no fuss about it, while she hurried to get the thing settled.

We boys would then earnestly watch Father while he ate the three chops.

Not that we didn't like Margaret's stew, which was the best in the world, but we regarded dinner as a special occasion, and we often had stew for lunch.

If some of us had taken up Father's offer, and left him with only one chop or none, I suppose that he would have asked Mother, "Where are the rest of the chops?" and been very cross about it when she told him there weren't any more. But his offer of them to us was sincere, though it cost him a struggle. He wanted plenty of food bought for everyone. His instincts were generous. Only, it made him cross if he suffered for those generous instincts.

Long after Margaret died, Father was speaking one night of how good her things always had tasted.

"I wish she could hear you," said Mother. She smiled tenderly at the thought of that gallant and dear little figure. "If anybody ever was sure of going to Heaven," she added, "I know it was Margaret."

This struck Father as a recommendation of the place. He took a sip of cognac and said casually, "I'll look her up when I get there. I'll have her take care of me."

Mother started to say something but checked herself.

"What's the matter?" he asked.

"Well, Clare dear," said Mother, "Margaret must be in some special part of Heaven, she was so good. You'd be very fortunate, Clare, to get to the same part as Margaret."

"Hah!" Father said, suddenly scowling. "I'll make a devil of a row if I don't."

CHAPTER 9

THE GIFT OF SONG

ONE DAY when I was about ten years old, and George eight, Father suddenly remembered an intention of his to have us taught music. There were numerous other things that he felt every boy ought to learn, such as swimming, blacking his own shoes, and bookkeeping; to say nothing of school work, in which he expected a boy to excel. He now recalled that music, too, should be included in our education. He held that all children should be taught to play on something, and sing.

He was right, perhaps. At any rate, there is a great deal to be said for his program. On the other hand, there are children and children. I had no ear for music.

Father was the last man to take this into consideration, however: he looked upon children as raw material that a father should mold. When I said I couldn't sing, he said nonsense. He went to the piano. He played a scale, cleared his throat, and sang *Do, re, mi,* and the rest. He did this with relish. He sang it again, high and low. He then turned to me and told me to sing it, too, which he accompanied me.

I was bashful. I again told him earnestly that I couldn't sing. He laughed. "What do *you* know about what you can or can't do?" And he added in a firm, kindly voice, "Do whatever I tell you." He was always so sure of himself that I couldn't help having faith in him. For all I knew, he could detect the existence of organs in a boy of which that boy had no evidence. It was astonishing, certainly, but if he said I could sing, I could sing.

I planted myself respectfully before him. He played the first note. He never wasted time in explanations; that was not his way; and I had only the dimmest understanding of what he wished me to do. But I struck out, haphazard, and chanted the extraordinary syllables loudly.

"No, no, no!" said Father, disgustedly.

We tried it again.

"No, no, no!" He struck the notes louder.

We tried it repeatedly. . . .

I gradually saw that I was supposed to match the piano, in some way, with my voice. But how such a thing could be done I had no notion whatever. The kind of sound a piano made was different from the sound of a voice. And the various notes—I could hear that each one had its own sound, but that didn't help me out any: they were all total strangers. One end of the piano made deep noises, the other end shrill; I could make my voice deep, shrill, or medium; but that was the best I could do.

At the end of what seemed to me an hour, I still stood at attention, while Father still tried energetically to force me to sing. It was an absolute deadlock. He wouldn't give in, and I couldn't. Two or three times I had felt for a moment I was getting the hang of it, but my voice wouldn't do what I wanted; I don't think it could. Anyhow, my momentary grasp of the problem soon faded. It felt so queer to be trying to do anything exact with my voice. And Father was so urgent about it, and the words so outlandish. *Do, re, mi, fa, sol, la, si, do!* What a nightmare! though by this time he had abandoned his insistence on my learning the scale; he had reduced his demands to my singing one single note: *Do.* I continually opened my mouth wide, as he had instructed me, and shouted the word

Do at random, hoping it might be the pitch. He snorted, and again struck the piano. I again shouted *Do*.

George sat on the sofa by the parlor door, watching me with great sympathy. He always had the easy end of it. George was a good brother; he looked up to me, loved me, and I couldn't help loving him; but I used to get tired of being his path-breaker in encounters with Father. All Father's experience as a parent was obtained at my hands. He was a man who had many impossible hopes for his children, and it was only as he tried these on me that he slowly became disillusioned. He clung to each hope tenaciously; he surrendered none without a long struggle; after which he felt baffled and indignant, and I felt done up, too. At such times if only he had repeated the attack on my brothers, it might have been hard on them but at least it would have given me a slight rest. But no, when he had had a disappointment, he turned to new projects. And as I was the eldest, the new were always tried out on me. George and the others trailed along happily, in comparative peace, while I perpetually confronted Father in a wrestling match upon some new ground. . . .

Mother came into the room in her long swishing skirts. Father was obstinately striking the piano for the nine thousandth time, and I was steadily though hopelessly calling out *Do*.

"Why Clare! What *are* you doing?" Mother cried.

Father jumped up. I suppose that at heart he was relieved at her interruption—it allowed him to stop without facing the fact of defeat. But he strongly wished to execute any such maneuver without loss of dignity, and Mother never showed enough regard for this, from his point of view. Besides, he was full of a natural irritation at the way things resisted him. He had visited only a part of this on me. The rest he now hurled at her. He said would she kindly go away and leave him alone with his sons. He declared he would not be interfered with. He banged the piano lid shut. He said he was "sick and tired of being systematically thwarted and hindered," and he swore he would be damned if he'd stand it. Off he went to his room.

"You'll only have to come right back down again," Mother called after him. "The soup's being put on the table."

"I don't want any dinner."

"Oh Clare! Please! it's oyster soup!"

"Don't want any." He slammed his room door.

We sat down, frightened, at table. I was exhausted. But the soup was a life-saver. It was more like a stew, really. Rich milk, oyster juice, and big oysters. I put lots of small hard crackers in mine, and one slice of French toast. That hot toast soaked in soup was delicious, only there wasn't much of it, and as Father particularly liked it, we had to leave it for him. But there was plenty of soup: a great tureen full. Each boy had two helpings.

Father came down in the middle of it, still offended, but he ate his full share. I guess he was somewhat in need of a life-saver himself. The chops and peas and potatoes came on. He gradually forgot how we'd wronged him.

There were too many things always happening at our family dinners, too many new vexations, or funny things, for him to dwell on the past.

But though he was willing enough, usually, to drop small resentments, nevertheless there were certain recollections that remained in his mind—such as the feeling that Mother sometimes failed to understand his plans for our welfare, and made his duty needlessly hard for him by her interference; and the impression that I was an awkward little boy, and great trouble to train.

Not that these thoughts disturbed him, or lessened at all his self-confidence. He lit his cigar after dinner and leaned back philosophically, taking deep vigorous puffs with enjoyment, and drinking black coffee. When I said, "Good night, Father," he smiled at me like a humorous potter, pausing to consider—for the moment—an odd bit of clay. Then he patted me affectionately on the shoulder and I went up to bed.

CHAPTER 10

THE NOBLEST
INSTRUMENT

FATHER HAD been away, reorganizing some old upstate railroad. He returned in an executive mood and proceeded to shake up our home. In spite of my failure as a singer, he was still bound to have us taught music. We boys were summoned before him and informed that we must at once learn to play on something. We might not appreciate it now, he said, but we should later on. "You, Clarence, will learn the violin. George, you the piano. Julian—well, Julian is too young yet. But you older boys must have lessons."

I was appalled at this order. At the age of ten it seemed a disaster to lose any more of my freedom. The days were already too short for our games after school; and now here was a chunk to come out of playtime three days every week. A chunk every day, we found afterward, because we had to practice.

George sat at the piano in the parlor, and faithfully learned to pound out his exercises. He had all the luck. He was not an inspired player, but at least he had some ear for music. He also had the advantage of playing on a good robust instrument, which he didn't have to be careful not to drop, and was in no danger of breaking. Furthermore, he did not have to tune it. A piano had some good points.

But I had to go through a blacker and more gruesome experience. It was bad enough to have to come in from the street and the sunlight and go down into our dark little basement where I took my lessons. But that was only the opening chill of the struggle that followed.

The whole thing was uncanny. The violin itself was a queer, fragile, cigar-boxy thing, that had to be handled most gingerly. Nothing sturdy about it. Why, a fellow was liable to crack it putting it into its case. And then my teacher, he was queer too. He had a queer pickled smell.

I dare say he wasn't queer at all really, but he seemed so to me, because he was different from the people I generally met. He was probably worth a dozen of some of them, but I didn't know it. He was one of the violins in the Philharmonic, and an excellent player; a grave, middle-aged little man—who was obliged to give lessons.

He wore a black, wrinkled frock coat, and a discolored gold watch-chain. He had small, black-rimmed glasses; not tortoise-shell, but thin rims of metal. His violin was dark, rich, and polished, and would do anything for him.

Mine was balky and awkward, brand new, and of a light, common color.

The violin is intended for persons with a passion for music. I wasn't that kind of person. I liked to hear a band play a tune that we could march up and down to, but try as I would, I could seldom whistle such a tune afterward. My teacher didn't know this. He greeted me as a possible genius.

He taught me how to hold the contraption, tucked under my chin. I learned how to move my fingers here and there on its handle or stem. I learned how to draw the bow across the strings, and thus produce sounds. . . .

Does a mother recall the first cry of her baby, I wonder? I still remember the strange cry at birth of that new violin.

My teacher, Herr M., looked as though he had suddenly taken a large glass of vinegar. He sucked in his breath. His lips were drawn back from his teeth, and his eyes tightly shut. Of course, he hadn't expected my notes to be sweet at the start; but still, there was something unearthly about that first cry. He snatched the violin from me, examined it, readjusted its pegs, and comforted it gently, by drawing his own bow across it. It was only a new and not especially fine violin, but the sounds it made for him were more natural—they were classifiable sounds. They were not richly musical, but at least they had been heard before on this earth.

He handed the instrument back to me with careful directions. I tucked it up under my chin again and grasped the end tight. I held my bow exactly as ordered. I looked up at him, waiting.

"Now," he said, nervously.

I slowly raised the bow, drew it downward. . . .

This time there were *two* dreadful cries in our little front basement. One came from my new violin and one from the heart of Herr M.

Herr M. presently came to, and smiled bravely at me, and said if I wanted to rest a moment he would permit it. He seemed to think I might wish to lie down awhile and recover. I didn't feel any need of lying down. All I wanted was to get through the lesson. But Herr M. was shaken. He was by no means ready to let me proceed. He looked around desperately, saw the music book, and said he would now show me that. We sat down side by side on the window-seat, with the book in his lap, while he pointed out the notes to me with his finger, and told me their names.

After a bit, when he felt better, he took up his own violin, and instructed me to watch him and note how he handled the strings. And then at last, he nerved himself to let me take my violin up again. "Softly, my child, softly," he begged me, and stood facing the wall. . . .

We got through the afternoon somehow, but it was a ghastly experience. Part of the time he was maddened by the mistakes I kept making, and part of the time he was plain wretched. He covered his eyes. He seemed ill. He looked often at his watch, even shook it as though it had stopped; but he stayed the full hour.

That was Wednesday. What struggles he had with himself before Friday, when my second lesson was due, I can only dimly imagine, and of course I never even gave them a thought at the time. He came back to recommence teaching me, but he had changed—he had hardened. Instead of being cross, he was stern; and instead of sad, bitter. He wasn't unkind to me, but we were no longer companions. He talked to himself, under his breath; and sometimes he took bits of paper, and did little sums on them, gloomily, and then tore them up.

During my third lesson I saw the tears come to his eyes. He went up to Father and said he was sorry but he honestly felt sure I'd never be able to play.

Father didn't like this at all. He said he felt sure I would. He dismissed Herr M. briefly—the poor man came stumbling back down in two minutes. In that short space of time he had gallantly gone upstairs in a glow, resolved upon sacrificing his earnings for the sake of telling the truth. He returned with his earnings still running, but with the look of a lost soul about him, as though he felt that his nerves and his sanity were doomed to destruction. He was low in his mind, and he talked to himself more than ever. Sometimes he spoke harshly of America, sometimes of fate.

But he no longer struggled. He accepted this thing as his destiny. He regarded me as an unfortunate something, outside the human species, whom he must simply try to labor with as well as he could. It was a grotesque, indeed a hellish experience, but he felt he must bear it.

He wasn't the only one—he was at least not alone in his sufferings. Mother, though expecting the worst, had tried to be hopeful about it, but at the end of a week or two I heard her and Margaret talking it over. I was slaughtering a scale in the front basement, when Mother came down and stood outside the door in the kitchen hall and whispered, "Oh, Margaret!"

I watched them. Margaret was baking a cake. She screwed up her
face, raised her arms, and brought them down with hands clenched.

"I don't know what we shall do, Margaret."

"The poor little feller," Margaret whispered. "He can't make the
thing go."

This made me indignant. They were making me look like a lub-
ber. I wished to feel always that I could make anything go. . . .

I now began to feel a determination to master this thing. History shows us many examples of the misplaced determinations of
men—they are one of the darkest aspects of human life, they spread
so much needless pain: but I knew little history. And I viewed what
little I did know romantically—I should have seen in such episodes
their heroism, not their futility. Any role that seemed heroic attracted
me, no matter how senseless.

Not that I saw any chance for heroism in our front basement,
of course. You had to have a battlefield or something. I saw only
that I was appearing ridiculous. But that stung my pride. I hadn't
wanted to learn anything whatever about fiddles or music, but since
I was in for it, I'd do it, and show them I could. A boy will often
put in enormous amounts of his time trying to prove he isn't as
ridiculous as he thinks people think him.

Meanwhile Herr M. and I had discovered that I was nearsighted.
On account of the violin's being an instrument that sticks out in
front of one, I couldn't stand close enough to the music book to see
the notes clearly. He didn't at first realize that I often made mistakes
from that cause. When he and I finally comprehended that I had
this defect, he had a sudden new hope that this might have been
the whole trouble, and that when it was corrected I might play like
a human being at last.

Neither of us ventured to take up this matter with Father. We
knew that it would have been hard to convince him that my eyes
were not perfect, I being a son of his and presumably made in his
image; and we knew that he immediately would have felt we were
trying to make trouble for him, and would have shown an amount

of resentment which it was best to avoid. So Herr M. instead lent me his glasses. These did fairly well. They turned the dim grayness of the notes into a queer bright distortion, but the main thing was they did make them brighter, so that I now saw more of them. How well I remember those little glasses. Poor, dingy old things. Herr M. was nervous about lending them to me; he feared that I'd drop them. It would have been safer if they had been spectacles: but no, they were pince-nez; and I had to learn to balance them across my nose as well as I could. I couldn't wear them up near my eyes because my nose was too thin there; I had to put them about half-way down where there was enough flesh to hold them. I also had to tilt my head back, for the music-stand was a little too tall for me. Herr M. sometimes mounted me on a stool, warning me not to step off. Then when I was all set, and when he without his glasses was blind, I would smash my way into the scales again.

All during the long winter months I worked away at this job. I gave no thought, of course, to the family. But they did to me. Our house was heated by a furnace, which had big warm air pipes; these ran up through the walls with wide outlets into each room, and sound traveled easily and ringingly through their roomy, tin passages. My violin could be heard in every part of the house. No one could settle down to anything while I was practicing. If visitors came they soon left. Mother couldn't even sing to the baby. She would wait, watching the clock, until my long hour of scale-work was over, and then come downstairs and shriek at me that my time was up. She would find me sawing away with my forehead wet, and my hair wet and stringy, and even my clothes slowly getting damp from my exertions. She would feel my collar, which was done for, and say I must change it. "Oh, Mother! Please!"—for I was in a hurry now to run out and play. But she wasn't being fussy about my collar, I can see, looking back; she was using it merely as a barometer or gauge of my pores. She thought I had better dry myself before going out in the snow.

It was a hard winter for Mother. I believe she also had fears for the baby. She sometimes pleaded with Father; but no one could ever tell Father anything. He continued to stand like a rock against stopping my lessons.

Schopenhauer, in his rules for debating, shows how to win a weak case by insidiously transferring an argument from its right field, and discussing it instead from some irrelevant but impregnable angle. Father knew nothing of Schopenhauer, and was never insidious, but, nevertheless, he had certain natural gifts for debate. In the first place his voice was powerful and stormy, and he let it out at full strength, and kept on letting it out with a vigor that stunned his opponents. As a second gift, he was convinced at all times that his opponents were wrong. Hence, even if they did win a point or two, it did them no good, for he dragged the issue to some other ground then, where he and Truth could prevail. When Mother said it surely was plain enough that I had no ear, what was his reply? Why, he said that the violin was the noblest instrument invented by man. Having silenced her with this solid premise he declared that it followed that any boy was lucky to be given the privilege of learning to play it. No boy should expect to learn it immediately. It required persistence. Everything, he had found, required persistence. The motto was, Never give up.

All his life, he declared, he had persevered in spite of discouragement, and he meant to keep on persevering, and he meant me to, too. He said that none of us realized what he had had to go through. If he had been the kind that gave up at the very first obstacle, where would he have been now—where would any of the family have been? The answer was, apparently, that we'd either have been in a very bad way, poking round for crusts in the gutter, or else nonexistent. We might have never even been born if Father had not persevered.

Placed beside this record of Father's vast trials overcome, the little difficulty of my learning to play the violin seemed a trifle. I faithfully spurred myself on again, to work at the puzzle. Even my teacher seemed impressed with these views on persistence. Though older than Father, he had certainly not made as much money, and he bowed to the experience of a practical man who was a success. If he, Herr M., had been a success he would not have had to teach boys; and sitting in this black pit in which his need of money had placed him, he saw more than ever that he must learn the ways of this world. He listened with all his heart, as to a god, when Father shook his forefinger, and told him how to climb to the heights where financial rewards were achieved. The idea he got was that perseverance was sure to lead to great wealth.

Consequently our front basement continued to be the home of lost causes.

Of course, I kept begging Herr M. to let me learn just one tune. Even though I seldom could whistle them, still I liked tunes; and I knew that, in my hours of practicing, a tune would be a comfort. That is, for myself. Here again I never gave a thought to the effect upon others.

Herr M., after many misgivings, to which I respectfully listened— though they were not spoken to me, they were muttered to himself, pessimistically—hunted through a worn old book of selections, and after much doubtful fumbling chose as simple a thing as he could find for me—for me and the neighbors.

It was spring now, and windows were open. That tune became famous.

What would the musician who had tenderly composed this air, years before, have felt if he had foreseen what an end it would have, on Madison Avenue; and how, before death, it would be execrated by that once peaceful neighborhood. I engraved it on their hearts; not in its true form but in my own eerie versions. It was the only tune I knew. Consequently I played and replayed it.

Even horrors when repeated grow old and lose part of their sting. But those I produced were, unluckily, never the same. To be sure, this tune kept its general structure the same, even in my sweating hands. There was always the place where I climbed unsteadily up to its peak, and that difficult spot where it wavered, or staggered, and stuck; and then a sudden jerk of resumption—I came out strong on that. Every afternoon when I got to that difficult spot, the neighbors dropped whatever they were doing to wait for that jerk, shrinking from the moment, and yet feverishly impatient for it to come.

But what made the tune and their anguish so different each day? I'll explain. The strings of a violin are wound at the end around pegs, and each peg must be screwed in and tightened till the string sounds just right. Herr M. left my violin properly tuned when he went. But suppose a string broke, or that somehow I jarred a peg loose. Its string then became slack and soundless. I had to re-tighten it. Not having an ear, I was highly uncertain about this.

Our neighbors never knew at what degree of tautness I'd put such a string. I didn't myself. I just screwed her up tight enough to make a strong reliable sound. Neither they nor I could tell which string would thus appear in a new role each day, nor foresee the profound transformations this would produce in that tune.

All that spring this unhappy and ill-destined melody floated out through my window, and writhed in the air for one hour daily, in sunshine or storm. All that spring our neighbors and I daily toiled to its peak, and staggered over its hump, so to speak, and fell wailing through space.

Things now began to be said to Mother which drove her to act. She explained to Father that the end had come at last. Absolutely. "This awful nightmare cannot go on," she said.

Father pooh-poohed her.

She cried. She told him what it was doing to her. He said that she was excited, and that her descriptions of the sounds I made were exaggerated and hysterical—must be. She was always too vehement, he shouted. She must learn to be calm.

"But you're downtown, *you* don't have to hear it!"

Father remained wholly skeptical.

She endeavored to shame him. She told him what awful things the neighbors were saying about him, because of the noise I was making, for which he was responsible.

He couldn't be made to look at it that way. If there really were any unpleasantness then I was responsible. He had provided me with a good teacher and a good violin—so he reasoned. In short, he had done his best, and no father could have done more. If I made hideous sounds after all that, the fault must be mine. He said that Mother should be stricter with me, if necessary, and make me try harder.

This was the last straw. I couldn't try harder. When Mother told me his verdict I said nothing, but my body rebelled. Self-discipline had its limits—and I wanted to be out: it was spring. I skimped my hours of practice when I heard the fellows playing outside. I came home late for lessons—even forgot them. Little by little they stopped.

Father was outraged. His final argument, I remember, was that my violin had cost twenty-five dollars; if I didn't learn it the money would be wasted, and he couldn't afford it. But it was put to him that my younger brother, Julian, could learn it instead, later on. Then summer came, anyhow, and we went for three months to the seashore; and in the confusion of this Father was defeated and I was set free.

In the autumn little Julian was led away one afternoon, and imprisoned in the front basement in my place. I don't remember how long they kept him down there, but it was several years. He had an ear, however, and I believe he learned to play fairly well. This would have made a happy ending for Herr M. after all; but it was some other teacher, a younger man, who was engaged to teach Julian. Father said Herr M. was a failure.

CHAPTER 11

FATHER TRIES TO MAKE MOTHER LIKE FIGURES

FATHER WAS always trying to make Mother keep track of the household expenses. He was systematic by nature and he had had a sound business training. He had a full set of account books at home in addition to those in his office—a personal cash-book, journal, and ledger—in which he carefully made double entries. His home ledger showed at a glance exactly how much a month or a year his clothes or his clubs or his cigar bills amounted to. Every item was listed. He knew just how every one of his expenses compared with those of former years, and when he allowed the figures to mount up in one place, he could bring them down in another.

Before he got married, these books had apparently given him great satisfaction, but he said they were never the same after that. They had suddenly stopped telling him anything. He still knew what his personal expenses were, but they were microscopic compared to his household expenses, and of those he knew nothing, no details, only the horrible total. His money was flowing away in all directions and he had no record of it.

Every once in so often he tried to explain his system to Mother. But his stout, leather-bound ledgers, and his methodical ruling of lines in red ink, and the whole business of putting down every little expense every day, were too much for her. She didn't feel that women should have anything to do with accounts, any more than men should have to see that the parlor was dusted. She had been only a débutante when she married, not long out of school, and though she had been head of her class, and wrote well and spelled well, and spoke beautiful French, she had never laid eyes on a ledger. Every time Father showed her his, she was unsympathetic.

Figures were so absorbing to Father that for a long time he couldn't believe Mother really disliked them. He hoped for years that her lack of interest was due only to her youth and that she would outgrow it. He said confidently that she would soon learn to keep books. It was simple. Meanwhile, if she would just make a memorandum for him of whatever she spent, he would enter it himself in the accounts until he could trust her to do it.

That day never arrived.

Father knew where some of the money went, for part of the expenses were charged. But this was a poor consolation. Although the household bills gave him plenty of data which he could sit and stare at, in horror, he said that many of the details were not clear to him, and most of the rest were incredible.

He tried to go over the bills regularly with Mother, as well as he could, demanding information about items which he did not understand. But every now and then there were items which she didn't understand, either. She said she wasn't sure they were mistakes, but she couldn't remember about them. Her mind was a blank. She behaved as though the bill were a total stranger to her.

This was one of the features that annoyed Father most.

Mother didn't like these sessions a bit. She told us she hated bills, anyhow. When they were larger than she expected, she felt guilty and hardly dared to let Father see them. When some of them seemed small to her, she felt happy, but not for long, because they never seemed small to Father. And when she spotted an error—when she found, for instance, that Tyson, the butcher, had charged too much for a broiler—she had to fly around to the shop to have it corrected, and argue it out, and go through a disagreeable experience, and then when she told Father how hard she had worked he took it as a matter of course, and she indignantly found that she never got any credit for it.

Sometimes I had to do this kind of thing, too. There was a man named Flannagan over on Sixth Avenue who supplied us with newspapers, and I used to be sent to rebuke him when he overcharged. Father said Flannagan had no head for figures. After checking up the addition and recomputing the individual items, he would generally discover that the bill was anywhere from three to fourteen cents out. He then sent for me, handed me the correct amount of change and the bill, and told me to go over to see Flannagan the next day, after school, and warn him that we wouldn't stand it.

I got used to this after a while, but the first time I went I was frightened. Flannagan was a large man who looked like a barkeeper and whose face was tough and belligerent. When I marched into his dark little shop and shakily attempted to warn him that we wouldn't stand it, he leaned over the counter, stared down at me, and said loudly, "Har?"

"Excuse me, Mr. Flannagan," I repeated, "here is your bill but it's wrong."

"*Har?*"

"It seems to be just a little wrong, sir. Eight cents too much for the *Sun.*"

Flannagan snatched the bill from me and the money, and went to his desk. After working over it with a thick pencil, and smudging the bill all up, front and back, he snarled to himself, and receipted it the way Father wished. Then he chucked it disdainfully on the counter. I picked it up and got out.

"Confound it all," Father said when he got it, "don't muss my bills up so."

"It was Mr. Flannagan, Father."

"Well, tell him he must learn to be tidy."

"Yes, sir," I said, hopelessly.

I liked figures myself, just as Father did, and I thought it was queer Mother didn't. She was as quick at them as anybody, yet she didn't get any fun out of writing them down and adding them up. I liked the problems in my school arithmetic, and I deeply admired Father's account books. I didn't dare tell him this, somehow. He never offered to let me examine those big, handsome books. He kept them locked up in a desk he had, down in the front basement.

If I showed Father one of my arithmetic lessons, he was interested—he got up from his chair and put down his newspaper and sat at the dining-room table with a pencil and paper, to see how well I had done. But Mother didn't want to go into such matters.

Every month when the bills came in, there was trouble. Mother seemed to have no great extravagances. But she loved pretty things. She had a passion for china, for instance. She saw hundreds of beautiful cups and saucers that it was hard to walk away from and leave. She knew she couldn't buy them, and mustn't, but every so often she did. No one purchase seemed large by itself, but they kept mounting up, and Father declared that she bought more china than the Windsor Hotel.

Father couldn't see why charge accounts should be a temptation to Mother. They were no temptation to him. He knew that the bill would arrive on the first of the month and that in a few days he would pay it. He said he had supposed that Mother would have the same feelings that he had about this.

But Mother was one of those persons for whom charge accounts were invented. When she bought something and charged it, the first of the next month seemed far away, and she hoped that perhaps Father wouldn't mind—he might be nice about it for once. Her desire for the thing was strong at that moment, the penalty was remote, and she fell.

She was a different woman entirely when she had to pay cash. It was hard to get cash out of Father, she never got much at one time, and as she looked in her pocketbook she could see her precious little hoard dwindling. She fingered a purchase and thought twice about it before she could bear to part with the money. But shopping on a charge account was fun. She tried not to let herself be tempted, but of course she was, all the time, and after she had conscientiously resisted nine lovely temptations, it didn't seem really wicked to yield to the tenth.

Father did his level best to take all the fun out of it for her. Once every month regularly he held court and sat as a judge, and required her to explain her crimes and misdemeanors. When she cried, or showed that she was hurt, it appeared that Father, too, felt hurt and worried. He said again and again at the top of his voice that he wished to be reasonable but that he couldn't afford to spend money that way, and that they would have to do better.

Once in a while when Father got low in his mind and said that he was discouraged, Mother felt so sorry that she tried hard to keep count of the cash for him. She put down all sorts of little expenses, on backs of envelopes or on half-sheets of letter paper of different sizes, and she gave these to Father with many interlineations and much scratching out of other memoranda, and with mystifying omissions. He would pore over them, calling out to her to tell him what this was, or that, in a vain attempt to bring order out of this feminine chaos.

Mother could sometimes, though not very often, be managed by praise, but criticism made her rebellious, and after a dose of it she wouldn't put down any figures at all for a while. She had to do the mending and marketing and take care of the children, and she told Father she had no time to learn to be a bookkeeper too. What was the use of keeping track of anything that was over and done with? She said that wasn't her way of doing things.

"Well," Father said patiently, "let's get at the bottom of this, now, and work out some solution. What *is* your way of doing things? Tell me."

Mother said firmly that her way was to do the very best she could to keep down expenses, and that all her friends thought she did wonderfully, and the Wards spend twice as much.

Father said, "Damn the Wards! They don't have to work for it. I don't wish to be told what they spend, or how they throw money around."

Mother said, "Oh, Clare, how can you! They don't. They just like to have things go nicely, and live in a comfortable way, and I thought you were so fond of Cousin Mary. You know very well she is lovely, and she gave the baby a cup."

Father declared that he might be fond of Cousin Mary without wanting to hear so damned much about her. He said she cropped up every minute.

"You talk of your own family enough," Mother answered.

Father felt this was very unjust. When he talked of his own family he criticized them, and as severely as he knew how. He held tightly onto himself in an effort to keep to the subject. He said that the point he was trying to make was that Cousin Mary's ways were not his ways, and that consequently there was no use whatever discussing them with him.

Mother said, "Goodness knows *I* don't want to discuss things, it's always you who are doing it, and if I can't even *speak* of Cousin Mary—"

"You can, you can speak of her all you want to," Father hotly protested. "But I won't have Cousin Mary or anyone else dictating to me how to run things."

"I didn't say a word about her dictating, Clare. She isn't that kind."

"I don't know what you said, now," Father replied. "You never stick to the point. But you implied in some way that Cousin Mary—"

"Oh, Clare, please! I didn't! And I can't bear to have you talk so harshly of her when she admires you so."

Something like this happened to every financial conversation they had. Father did his best to confine the discussion to the question at issue, but somehow, no matter how calmly he started, he soon got exasperated and went galloping fiercely off in any direction Mother's mind happened to take; and in the middle of it one of the babies would cry and Mother would have to go off to see what was wrong, or she would have to run down to leave word for Mrs. Tobin, the washerwoman, to do Father's shirts differently, and when Father complained Mother reminded him reproachfully that she had to keep house.

Father was baffled by these tactics. But every time he went back down to the basement and ruled neat lines in his ledgers, he made up his mind all over again that he wouldn't give up.

CHAPTER 12

FATHER AND HIS HARD-ROCKING SHIP

FATHER SAID that one great mystery about the monthly household expenses was what made them jump up and down so. "Anyone would suppose that there would be some regularity after a while which would let a man try to make plans, but I never know from one month to another what to expect."

Mother said she didn't, either. Things just seemed to go that way.

"But they have no business to go that way, Vinnie," Father declared. "And what's more I won't allow it."

Mother said she didn't see what she could do about it. All she knew was that when the bills mounted up, it didn't mean that she had been extravagant.

"Well, it certainly means that you've spent a devil of a lot of money," said Father.

Mother looked at him obstinately. She couldn't exactly deny this, but she said that it wasn't fair.

Appearances were often hopelessly against Mother but that never daunted her. She wasn't afraid of Father or anybody. She was a woman of great spirit who would have flown at and pecked any tyrant. It was only when she had a bad conscience that she had no heart to fight. Father had the best of her there because he never had a bad conscience. And he didn't know that he was a tyrant. He regarded himself as a long-suffering man who asked little of anybody, and who showed only the greatest moderation in his encounters with unreasonable beings like Mother. Mother's one advantage over him was that she was quicker. She was particularly elusive when Father was trying to hammer her into shape.

When the household expenses shot up very high, Father got frightened. He would then, as Mother put it, yell his head off. He always did some yelling anyhow, merely on general principles, but when his alarm was genuine he roared in real anguish.

Usually this brought the total down again, at least for a while. But there were times when no amount of noise seemed to do any good, and when every month for one reason or another the total went on up and up. And then, just as Father had almost resigned himself to this awful outgo, and just as he had eased up on his yelling and had begun to feel grim, the expenses, to his utter amazement, would take a sharp drop.

Mother didn't keep track of these totals, she was too busy watching small details, and Father never knew whether to tell her the good news or not. He always did tell her, because he couldn't keep things to himself. But he always had cause to regret it.

When he told her, he did it in as disciplinary a manner as possible. He didn't congratulate her on the expenses having come down. He appeared at her door, waving the bills at her with a threatening scowl, and said, "I've told you again and again that you could keep the expenses down if you tried, and this shows I was right."

Mother was always startled at such attacks, but she didn't lose her presence of mind. She asked how much less the amount was and said it was all due to her good management, of course, and Father ought to give her the difference.

At this point Father suddenly found himself on the defensive and the entire moral lecture that he had intended to deliver was wrecked. The more they talked, the clearer it seemed to Mother that he owed her that money. Only when he was lucky could he get out of her room without paying it.

He said that this was one of the things about her that was enough to drive a man mad.

The other thing was her lack of system, which was always cropping up in new ways. He sometimes looked at Mother as though he had never seen her before. "Upon my soul," he said, "I almost believe you don't know what system is. You don't even want to know, either."

He had at last invented what seemed a perfect method of recording expenses. Whenever he gave any money to Mother, he asked her what it was for and made a note of it in his pocket notebook. His idea was that these items, added to those in the itemized bills, would show him exactly where every dollar had gone.

But they didn't.

He consulted his notebook. "I gave you six dollars in cash on the twenty-fifth of last month," he said, "to buy a new coffeepot."

"Yes," Mother said, "because you broke your old one. You threw it right on the floor."

Father frowned. "I'm not talking about that," he answered. "I am simply endeavoring to find out from you, if I can—"

"But it's so silly to break a nice coffeepot, Clare, and that was the last of those French ones, and there was nothing the matter with the coffee that morning; it was made just the same as it always is."

"It wasn't," said Father. "It was made in a damned barbaric manner."

"And I couldn't get another French one," Mother continued, "because that little shop the Auffmordts told us about has stopped selling them. They said the tariff wouldn't let them any more, and I told Monsieur Duval he ought to be ashamed of himself to stand there and say so. I said that if I had a shop, I'd like to see the tariff keep me from selling things."

"But I gave you six dollars to buy a new pot," Father firmly repeated, "and now I find that you apparently got one at Lewis & Conger's and charged it. Here's their bill: 'one brown earthenware drip coffeepot, five dollars.'"

"So I saved you a dollar," Mother triumphantly said, "and you can hand it right over to me."

"Bah! What nonsense you talk!" Father cried. "Is there no way to get this thing straightened out? What did you do with the six dollars?"

"Why, Clare! I can't tell you now, dear. Why didn't you ask at the time?"

"Oh, my God!" Father groaned.

"Wait a moment," said Mother. "I spent four dollars and a half for that new umbrella I told you I wanted, and you said I didn't need a new one, but I did, very much."

Father got out his pencil and wrote "New Umbrella for V." in his notebook.

"And that must have been the week," Mother went on, "that I paid Mrs. Tobin for two extra days' washing, so that was two dollars more out of it, which makes it six-fifty. There's another fifty cents that you owe me."

"I don't owe you anything," Father said. "You have managed to turn a coffeepot for me into a new umbrella for you. No matter what I give you money for, you buy something else with it, and if this is to keep on, I might as well not keep account books at all."

"I'd like to see you run this house without having any money on hand for things," Mother said.

"I am not made of money," Father replied. "You seem to think I only have to put my hand in my pocket to get some."

Mother not only thought this, she knew it. His wallet always was full. That was the provoking part of it—she knew he had the money right there, but he tried to keep from giving it to her. She had to argue it out of him.

"Well, you can put your hand in your pocket and give me that dollar-fifty this minute," she said. "You owe me that, anyhow."

Father said he didn't have a dollar-fifty to spare and tried to get back to his desk, but Mother wouldn't let him go till he paid her. She said she wouldn't put up with injustice.

Mother said it hampered her dreadfully never to have any cash. She was always having to pay out small amounts for demands that she had forgot to provide for, and in such emergencies the only way to do was to juggle things around. One result, however, of all these more or less innocent shifts was that in this way she usually took care of all her follies herself. All the small ones, at any rate. They never got entered on Father's books, except when they were monstrous.

She came home one late afternoon in a terrible state. "Has it come yet?" she asked the waitress.

The waitress said nothing had come that she knew of.

Mother ran upstairs with a hunted expression and flung herself down on her bed. When we looked in, she was sobbing.

It turned out that she had gone to an auction, and she had become so excited that she had bought but not paid for a grandfather's clock.

Mother knew in her heart that she had no business going to auctions. She was too suggestible, and if an hypnotic auctioneer once got her eye, she was lost. Besides, an auction aroused all her worst instincts—her combativeness, her recklessness, and her avaricious love of a bargain. And the worst of it was that this time it wasn't a bargain at all. At least she didn't think it was now. The awful old thing was about eight feet tall, and it wasn't the one she had wanted. It wasn't half as nice as the clock that old Miss Van Derwent had bought. And inside the hood over the dial, she said, there was a little ship which at first she hadn't noticed, a horrid ship that rocked up and down every time the clock ticked. It made her ill just to look at it. And she didn't have the money, and the man said he'd have to send it this evening, and what would Father say?

She came down to dinner, and left half-way through. Couldn't stand it. But an hour or two later, when the doorbell rang, she bravely went to tell Father.

She could hardly believe it, but she found that luck was with her, for once. If the clock had come earlier, there might have been a major catastrophe, but Father was in a good mood and he had had a good dinner. And though he never admitted it or spoke of it, he had a weakness for clocks. There were clocks all over the house, which he would allow no one to wind but himself. Every Sunday between breakfast and church he made the rounds, setting them at the right time by his infallible watch, regulating their speed, and telling us about every clock's little idiosyncrasies. When he happened to be coming downstairs on the hour, he cocked his ear, watch in hand, to listen to as many of them as he could, in the hope that they would all strike at once. He would reprove the impulsive pink clock in the spare room for striking too soon, and the big solemn clock in the dining-room for being a minute too late.

So when Mother led him out in the hall to confess to him and show him what she had bought, and he saw it was a clock, he fell in love with it, and made almost no fuss at all.

The let-down was too much for Mother. She tottered off to her room without another word and went straight to bed, leaving Father and the auctioneer's man setting up the new clock alongside the hatrack. Father was especially fascinated by the hard-rocking ship.

CHAPTER 13

FATHER HAS TROUBLE
WITH THE LAND OF
EGYPT

ONE WINTER when most of us boys were away, Mother was invited to go to Egypt with Mrs. Tytus and two or three others. Mrs. Tytus's son, Bob, was in charge of the party. They were going to sail up the Nile in a houseboat, they would see Luxor and Memphis, and altogether it seemed to be an ideal opportunity. Mother loved travel. She was eager to see any place that was new to her, even a place that was comparatively near-by like the Whitneys' camp up in Maine, and as Egypt was ten times as far away it seemed ten times as attractive.

She explained to Father what a wonderful chance it was. He was not impressed. He said she wanted to go anywhere, always, and he had never seen such a woman. Most women were glad to have a home, he said, and knew enough to appreciate it, but the only thing Mother seemed to want was to be on the go.

He went on to say that he himself had some sense, however, and that he would no more think of going to Egypt than to the North

Pole. In a year or two, if he could get away from business, they might go to London and Paris once more, but not one of the Day family had ever even set foot in Egypt, and nobody else he knew had, either, except Charlie Bond, who was one of those restless fellows anyhow and was always doing queer things. He said it was a wild and entirely unsuitable country, and that never in any circumstances whatever would he take Mother to Egypt.

"But that's just why I want to go, Clare, dear. You don't understand."

Father stared at her, and said, "What! What's why you want to go? Of course I don't understand."

"Why, because you don't like it. I thought it would please you."

The veins in Father's forehead began to swell. "You thought it would *please* me?"

"Oh Clare, dear, don't be stupid. I knew you wouldn't want to take me over to Egypt yourself, but don't you see, if Mrs. Tytus takes me, you won't ever have to."

This theory that Mother was only trying to save him trouble by getting on a ship and going to Egypt completely dumbfounded Father. But Mother clung firmly to it. She said of course she hated to have him miss seeing the Pyramids, but still she wouldn't enjoy dragging him off there if he was so unwilling, so he could just stay home and be comfortable in his own way while she went quietly over with Mrs. Tytus and hurried straight back.

To help clinch the matter, she brought Mrs. Tytus to see him. She brought young Bob Tytus too. She told Father how much her letter of credit should be, and when he protested, she said she was saving him money, because it would be nearly twice as much if he took her himself.

When Father said violently that he wished her to remain at his side, she said everybody had to go away sometimes, and Dr. Markoe had warned her she must.

Dr. Markoe was a man Father liked. Mrs. Tytus was tactful and beautiful. Mother was pertinacious. Between them all, they actually bore Father down, and on the appointed day Mother got aboard the ship, letter of credit and all, with Father swearing that now he would have to worry about her all winter, and he wouldn't be happy for a minute until she got back.

"Goodbye, darling," she said. "Do be quiet and nice while I'm gone."

"I won't!" he shouted, kissing her, and he marched stiffly off, saying, "I hope you are satisfied," and then turned back at the foot of the gangplank, calling loudly, "Dear Vinnie!" Mother waved her hand, the whistles blew hoarsely, and the crowds swirled and jostled, hiding these two from each other as the ship slid away.

Father began looking for letters the very next morning, and when none came he cursed the pilot and the postman, and said that he had a bad headache. But a letter did arrive in a few days, when the pilot had had time to mail it, and after the first three or four weeks we heard from Mother often.

Some of the letters told us how she was constantly meeting people she knew, not only on the ship but at every port where Mrs. Tytus and she went ashore. "Your mother has the damnedest number of friends I ever heard of," said Father. "She's everlastingly meeting some old friend or other wherever she goes. I never see people I know when I'm traveling. But there isn't a city in Europe where your mother wouldn't spot a friend in five minutes." And when a letter came saying she had just climbed Mt. Vesuvius and had found old Mr. and Mrs. Quintard of Rye at the top, peering down into the crater, Father said that upon his soul he never knew anyone like her.

Other letters were full of household advice and instructions about menus, or warnings to Father to keep an eye on the rubber tree and to speak about washing the curtains. Others abused the bad habits of foreigners and the inconveniences and troubles she met. "Well, why doesn't she stay home, then?" Father demanded triumphantly. Though he swore at every foreigner who dared to inconvenience her, he relished the complaints in these letters.

But when Mother left civilization behind her, even a far outpost like Cairo, and went off up the Nile in a thing called a dahabeah, manned by native boatmen, and when letters came from queer-sounding ancient cities in the interior, Father got nervous. He said it was a wild, harum-scarum thing to do. Moreover, it was entirely needless. He said he could see all of Egypt he wanted to without leaving New York—there were enough musty old mummies in the Museum to satisfy anybody. "But your mother wouldn't look at them; no, they weren't dead enough for her; she had to go traipsing off to see a mummy on its native heath. Why, somebody even brought an obelisk over here at great expense," he went on, "and left it to crumble away in the Park, where people can see it for nothing, but for some reason or other it isn't crumbly enough for your mother."

There were letters about the strange range of hills back of Thebes, and the great colonnades at Karnak, and the statues and tombs, which Father pished at impatiently; and there were letters about fleas, and moonlight and Nubian songs, and finally letters with snapshots. Father said he hated these photographs. He spent a great deal of time staring at them in deep disapproval. There was one in particular of Mother looking very roguish and chic in her voluminous dress, sitting way up on top of a tall and insolent camel, with two big black men in white turbans standing off at one side. No other member of the party around. Not a soul in sight but the black men and Mother. Father looked at that photograph often and groaned about it at night, and kept shouting things to himself about "the ends of the earth."

Soon after that, Mother turned around and headed for home. Father grew more and more eager to have her back, every day. Up to this time he had been comparatively quiet, for him, but the nearer the day of her return came the more noisy and impatient he got. Even at the pier, he made indignant remarks about how slow the ship was, getting in.

He forgot this mood, however, the minute he hugged her, and he instantly took charge of her things—all except her black bag, which she would never let anyone touch—and he ordered all the customs inspectors around and got Mother through in a jiffy, and he found a man to shoulder her trunk and he picked out the best hackman, and as the carriage rattled off over the cobblestones, Mother said she was glad to be back.

Father had taken particular pains to have everything in the house in its place, so that when Mother came in the door, she would say that home was just the way she had left it. Instead, what she actually said was "Oh, this poor room! Why, I never!" and she put down the black bag and began setting the chairs at different angles and moving her favorite ornaments affectionately as she straightened them out. "Poor things," she said, as she patted them, "didn't anybody know enough to turn you around the way you belong?" Father followed her, looking puzzled at these minute changes, and calling her attention to the rubber tree, which had grown half a foot. "Well," Mother said, "of all the forlorn objects, with those dead leaves left hanging there!" But when Father's face fell and she saw how disappointed he looked, she smiled at him to console him and said, "You did the best you could, darling." And she climbed upstairs to unpack.

The letter of credit had been very much on Father's mind. He had never before given Mother the management of any such sum. He was so happy to have her back that he said nothing about this at first. He was waiting for Mother to speak of it. But she said nothing either.

He had two expectations about it, and he didn't know which to trust. One was hopeful but slightly unreal. The other, based on long experience, was pessimistic.

It had been a large letter of credit, not as much as Mrs. Tytus had recommended but still, he felt, generous. He felt he had a right to expect that Mother hadn't spent all of it, but had left a substantial balance undrawn which he could now restore to his bank account. His other and realer expectation was that she had spent every cent and had possibly even had to borrow from Mrs. Tytus besides. The fact that she was avoiding the subject pointed to this latter outcome.

One night, after she had gone up to bed, she came back down for a moment to hand him some papers. "You might be going over these, Clare," she said. "I couldn't keep track of everything for you; I tried my best but I couldn't. But I saved all the bills." And she went off to bed again.

Father checked them over, one by one, carefully. They were full of strange-looking details:

CAIRO, FEB. 24, 1900.

MRS. DAY,
    Room 195,
        Shepheard's Hotel.

To 1 Passage to Second Cataract	£ 23. 0.0.
To 60 days on Dahabeah Tih	85.16.0.
	£ 108.16.0.

"Second Cataract!" Father muttered to himself vehemently. What would such a woman do next?

These bills supplied Father with more details than he had hoped to keep track of, and there was none of them that he felt much inclined to dispute. But as there were still several hundred dollars unaccounted for, he waited for Mother to confess what she had done with the balance.

Day after day went by without her saying one word. He began to fear that things must be serious. He became so alarmed that it would have been a relief to him to know the worst and be done with it. But do what he could—without direct questioning—he could get nothing out of her.

Mother had noticed him fumbling hints of course, and she did have a confession to make. But first she went and had a long talk with a young girl she was fond of—a girl whose name was Wilhelmine Johnson, whom George afterward married. Mother confided to Wilhelmine in secret that the situation was this: she hadn't spent all her letter of credit but she hated to give up the balance. It was wicked of her to feel that way, she supposed, but she meant to keep it herself.

Wilhelmine instantly took a strong stand about this. She said that on no account should Mother hand over that money to Father. Mother had always wanted to have some money of her own, Wilhelmine reminded her, and now here was her chance.

As Mother listened to this advice she felt happy, but she also felt frightened. It seemed to her far more daring to hang onto that money than it had been to ride on a camel. But while she was away all those months she had had a taste of what independence was like, and she was reluctant to drop back into her Victorian role.

When at last she nerved herself to tell Father, he felt better at once, but he smilingly reproved her for not having come to him sooner; and as to her keeping the money he said that that was all nonsense. He said that she was home now, thank God, and as he always paid all her bills at home she had no use for this money.

"Yes I have too," Mother said.

"Well, what will you use it for, then?" Father asked.

Mother didn't wish to explain. As a matter of fact she had no very definite ideas as to what she wanted some cash of her own for— she only knew that she wanted it. She said: "Oh, there are lots of little things I could use it for, Clare. Things I'd like to get when I need them, without so much talk."

This seemed unconvincing to Father. He demanded the balance. He felt that he was the natural custodian of any such fund and the only safe place for it was in his bank account, as Mother, of course, didn't have one. But Mother insisted on hiding it away in her own bureau drawer. Father pointed out how reckless this was, but he could do nothing with her. That voyage to Egypt had changed her; she was always much harder to manage after that sail up the Nile.

As a gracious concession, however, she presented Father with a large pale blue scarab, mounted to use as a scarfpin, which she said she hadn't really meant to let him have until Christmas. Father looked at this object without enthusiasm and asked what it was. When he was told that it was the image of a sacred beetle, he immediately pushed it away. He didn't want any dead beetles in his scarf, he declared. He told Mother she could send it right back to the tomb it had come from. He said that he begged to inform her that he was not a mummy.

CHAPTER 14

FATHER TEACHES ME TO BE PROMPT

FATHER MADE a great point of our getting down to breakfast on time. I meant to be prompt, but it never occurred to me that I had better try to be early. My idea was to slide into the room at the last moment. Consequently, I often was late.

My brothers were often late, too, with the exception of George. He was the only thoroughly reliable son Father had. George got down so early, Father pointed out to me, that he even had time to practice a few minutes on the piano.

The reason George was so prompt was that he was in a hurry to see the sporting page before Father got hold of the newspaper, and the reason he then played the piano was to signal to the rest of us, as we dressed, which team had won yesterday's ball game. He had made up a code for this purpose, and we leaned over the banisters, pulling on our stockings and shoes, to hear him announce the results. I don't remember now what the titles were of the airs he selected, but the general idea was that if he played a gay, lively air it meant that the Giants had won, and when the strains of a dirge or lament floated up to us, it meant that Pop Anson had beaten them.

As Father didn't approve of professional baseball, we said nothing to him about this arrangement. He led his life and we led ours, under his nose. He took the newspaper away from George the moment he entered the room, and George said good morning to him and stepped innocently into the parlor. Then, while Father watched him through the broad doorway and looked over the political headlines, George banged out the baseball news for us on the piano. Father used to admonish him with a chuckle not to thump it so hard, but George felt that he had to. We were at the top of the house, and he wanted to be sure that we'd hear him even if we were brushing our teeth. George always was thorough about things. He not only thumped the piano as hard as he could but he hammered out the tune over and over besides, while Father impatiently muttered to himself, *"Trop de zèle."*

Upstairs, there was usually some discussion as to what kind of news George was sending. He had not been allowed to learn popular tunes, which it would have been easy for us to recognize, and the few classic selections which were available in his little music book sounded pretty much alike at a distance. George rendered these with plenty of good will and muscle but not a great deal of sympathy. He regarded some of the rules of piano-playing as needlessly complicated.

The fact remained that he was the one boy who was always on time, and Father was so pleased by this that he bought a watch for him with "George Parmly Day, Always on Time" engraved on the back. He told me that as I was the eldest he had meant to give me a watch first, and he showed me the one he had bought for me. It was just like George's except that nothing had been engraved on it yet. Father explained that to his regret he would have to put it away for a while, until I had earned it by getting down early to breakfast.

Time went on, without much improvement on my part. Dawdling had got to be a habit with me. Sometimes my lateness was serious.

One morning, when breakfast was half over and I had nothing on but a pair of long woolen drawers, Father called up from the front hall, napkin in hand, that he wouldn't stand it and that I was to come down that instant. When I shouted indignantly that I wasn't dressed yet, he said he didn't care. "Come down just as you are, confound it!" he roared. I was tempted to take him at his word, but thought there might be some catch in it and wouldn't, though I hurried, of course, all I could. Father ate his usual hearty breakfast in a stormy mood, and I ate my usual hearty breakfast in a guilty and nervous one. Come what might, we always ate heartily. I sometimes wished afterward that I hadn't, but it never seemed to hurt Father.

Mother told Father that if he would give me the watch, she was sure I'd do better. He said that he didn't believe it, and that that was a poor way to bring a boy up. To prove to him that he was wrong, Mother at last unlocked her jewel box and gave me a watch which had belonged to one of her elderly cousins. It was really too valuable a watch for a boy to wear, she said, and I must be very careful of it. I promised I would.

This watch, however, turned out to be painfully delicate. It was old, I was young. We were not exactly made for each other. It had a back and front of thin gold, and as a Mother had had the former owner's monogram shaved off the front cover, that cover used to sink in the middle when pressed. Also, the lid fitted so closely that there was barely room for the glass crystal over the face. Such a very thin crystal had to be used that any pressure on the lid broke it.

I didn't press on the lid, naturally, after the first time this happened. I was careful, and everything would have gone well enough if other boys had been careful, too. It was not practicable, however, for me to make them be careful enough. When I had a fight, friendly or otherwise, I used to ask my opponent if he would be so kind as not to punch me on the left side of my stomach. He might or might not listen. If he and I were too excited and kept on long enough, the watch crystal broke anyway. There was never time to take off my watch first, and anyhow there was no place to put it. A watch that goes around the streets in a boy's pocket has to take life as it comes. This watch had never been designed for any such fate.

The first two crystals I broke Mother paid for, as Father disapproved of the whole business and would have nothing to do with it. Mother was always short of small change, however, and I hated to trouble her—and she hated to be troubled, too. "Oh, Clarence, dear! You haven't broken your watch again?" she cried when I opened the cover the second time, to show her the shattered fragments. She was so upset that I felt too guilty to tell her the next time it happened, and from then on I was reduced to the necessity of paying for the damage myself.

My pocket money never exceeded a dollar a month. Every new crystal cost twenty-five cents. It was a serious drain.

Wrestling and rolling around on the floor with Sam Willets, my watch quite forgotten, I would suddenly hear a faint tinkle and know that I was once more insolvent. I would pick out the broken glass and leave the watch with no crystal till I had twenty-five cents on hand, but these delays made me nervous. I knew that Mother wanted to feel sure I was taking good care of the watch, and that she might look at it any evening. As soon as I had the money, I hurried over to Sixth Avenue, where two old Germans kept a tiny watch shop, and left it there to be fixed. One of my most dismal memories is of that stuffy little shop's smell of sauerkraut, and how tall the glass counter then seemed, and the slowness of those two old Germans. When I got there late and they made me leave the watch overnight, I didn't have one easy moment until I got it back the next day. Again and again I argued with them that twenty-five cents was too much, especially for a regular customer, but they said it didn't pay them to do work even for that, because those thin old-fashioned crystals were hard to get.

I gave up at last. I told my Mother I didn't want to wear the watch any more.

Then I found, to my amazement, that this way out of my troubles was barred. The watch was an heirloom. And an heirloom was a thing that its recipient must value and cherish. No good Chinese, I read later on in life, fails to honor his ancestors; and no good boy, I was told in my youth, fails to appreciate heirlooms.

I left Mother's room in low spirits. That night, as I wound up my watch with its slender key, I envied George. Father had selected the right kind for George; he knew what a boy needed. It had a thick nickel case, it had an almost unbreakable crystal, and it endured daily life imperturbably, even when dropped in the bathtub.

It seemed to me that I was facing a pretty dark future. The curse of great possessions became a living thought to me, instead of a mere phrase. The demands that such possessions made on their owners for upkeep were merciless. For months I had had no money for marbles. I couldn't even afford a new top. In some way that I didn't fully understand I was yoked to a watch I now hated—a delicate thing that would always make trouble unless I learned to live gingerly.

Then I saw a way out. All this time I had kept on being late for breakfast at least once a week, out of habit, but it now occurred to me that if I could reform, perhaps Father might relent and give me that reliable nickel watch he had bought. I reformed. I occasionally weakened in my new resolution at first, but every time that crystal got broken I was spurred on to fresh efforts. When I had at length established a record for promptness that satisfied Father, he had my name engraved on the watch he had bought, and presented it to me. He was a little surprised at the intense pleasure I showed on this occasion, and as he watched me hopping around the room in delight he said "There, there" several times. "Don't be so excited, confound it," he added. "You'll knock over that vase."

Mother said she couldn't see why Father should give me a nickel watch when I had a gold one already, but he laughed and told her that "that old thing" was no kind of a watch for a boy. She reluctantly laid it away again to rest in her jewel box.

Her parting shot at Father was that anyhow she had been right; she had said all along that a watch was what I needed to teach me how to be prompt.

CHAPTER 15

FATHER INTEFERES WITH THE TWENTY-THIRD PSALM

WHEN WE boys were little, we used to go to Mother's room Sunday evenings, on our way upstairs to bed, and sit in a circle around her, while she told us a story from the Bible or talked to us about how good we ought to be and how much we ought to love God. She loved God herself as much as she dared to, and she deeply loved us, and she was especially tender and dear on those Sunday evenings. One of my brothers told me years afterward how much they had meant to him in those days, and how he had cherished the memory of them all his life.

I was a little older than my brothers, though, and my feelings were mixed. I loved Mother and hated to disappoint her, but I couldn't respond as easily as the other boys to her gentle appeals. I never seemed to have the emotions that she waited for me to show. I wish now that I could have listened uncritically and have thought only of the look in her eyes. What difference need it have made to me whether we had the same ideas about God, or whether the stories Mother thought lovely seemed less so to me? But there

I sat, staring uncomfortably at the carpet and trying to avoid answering questions.

One night she repeated the Twenty-third Psalm to us and asked us to learn it by heart. "The Lord is my shepherd," she whispered, softly. "He maketh me to lie down in green pastures: he leadeth me beside the still waters." She raised her eyes and went on bravely, although with a quiver of fear: "Thy rod and thy staff they comfort me." She had often felt the Lord's rod.

I heard Father going by in the hall. He looked in at the doorway and smiled affectionately at us and at Mother. Then he went off, and I heard his firm step as he walked on toward his room.

He hadn't meant to interfere with Mother's teachings. He hadn't spoken one word. But I found myself speculating, all of a sudden, on what his opinion would be of the Twenty-third Psalm.

I couldn't imagine Father being comforted by the Lord's rod and staff, or allowing anybody whatever to lead him to a pasture and get him to lie down somewhere in it. I could see him in my mind's eye, in his tailed coat and top hat, refusing point-blank even to enter a pasture. He would as soon have thought of wearing overalls. In spite of my admiring him for this attitude, it seemed wicked of him. I felt resentful about it. It would have been so much easier for me to be properly reverent if he had not been around. My idea was that if Mother was too religious, Father wasn't religious enough.

"Good night, Clarence," I heard Mother saying. "You won't forget, darling?"

I kissed her and went out, wondering what I was not to forget. Oh, yes—she had asked us to learn that psalm by heart.

Up in my bedroom, I got out my Bible. It was full of paper bookmarks, to help me find texts that I'd had to memorize, and these bookmarks in turn were full of pictures I had drawn of Biblical scenes. A picture of Adam looking doubtfully at the Tree of Knowledge in Eden, with a complete set of school books dangling heavily down from its boughs. A picture of Sarah "dealing hardly with

Hagar," driving her out with a broomstick. A picture of the sun, moon, and stars bowing politely to Joseph.

I sat down and added to the collection a picture of Job in pajamas, weeping copiously as he endeavored, on top of all his other trials, to learn the Twenty-third Psalm. I also drew his three unsatisfactory friends, sitting in a row staring at Job. Each friend wore a sardonic expression and had a large mustache and imperial like Napoleon the Third.

I got out another Bible that Mother had lent me. This one was in French, and it sometimes shocked me deeply to read it. As my belief was that when God had created the world He had said "Let there be light," it seemed to me highly irreverent to put French words in His mouth and have Him exclaim, *"Que la lumière soit!"* Imagine the Lord talking French! Aside from a few odd words in Hebrew, I took it completely for granted that God had never spoken anything but the most dignified English.

The French were notoriously godless, however. It made me laugh, though it frightened me, too, to see what liberties they had taken. In my English Bible, David was a fine Anglo-Saxon type, "a youth, ruddy and of a fair countenance." In the French, he was a revolting little snip from the boulevards, *"un enfant, blond, et d'une belle figure."* Where my Bible spoke of "leviathan," the French said *"le crocodile,"* which ruined the grandeur and mystery of that famous beast. And where mine said, "Behold now behemoth," they said, *"Voici l'hippopotame!"*

Instead of the children of Israel fearing lest the Lord should be wroth, the French said *"les enfants d'Israel"* were afraid lest *"le Seigneur"* should be *"irrité."*. This word *"irrité"* appeared everywhere in the French version. It wasn't only the Lord. Cain was *"très irrité."* Moïse (which seemed to me a very jaunty way of referring to Moses) was *"irrité"* again and again. Everybody was *"irrité."* When my regular Bible, the real one, impressively described men as "wroth," their anger seemed to have something stately and solemn about it. If they were full of mere irritation all the time, they were more like the Day family.

I turned at last to the Twenty-third Psalm. They had spoiled that, too. They had twisted it around until it read as though the scene were in Paris. "Green pastures" were changed into *"parcs herbeux,"* and "thy rod and thy staff" had become *"ton bâton,"* as though the Lord were leading David up and down the Bois de Boulogne like a drum major.

I decided to go to bed and let that psalm wait for a day or two. But before putting the books back on my shelf, I hunted up the one place in the French Bible that I really liked. "Blessed are the meek," my English Bible said, "for they shall inherit the earth." I had always hated that verse. It made all religion so difficult. Uriah Heep typified the meek, to my mind. The meek were a sniveling, despicable, and uncomfortable lot. But in poring over the French Bible one evening, I had found to my delight that some daring Frenchman had altered this passage, and had changed the Sermon on the Mount into something that a fellow could stand. *"Heureux les débonnaires,"* he had represented Jesus as saying, *"car ils hériteront de la terre."*

The debonair! That was more like it! I cheerfully jumped into bed.

CHAPTER 16

MOTHER AND THE ARMENIAN

MOTHER USED to take us boys to a summer resort in our vacations. In all such places there was usually an Armenian, prowling around the hotel piazza. Blue-black hair, dark skin, gleaming eyes, a hooked nose, perfect teeth. Mother said that there wasn't a lady on the piazza who didn't envy those teeth. The Armenian was always trying to catch the eye of one of them to see if he couldn't persuade her to look at his rugs or his silks. "Not buy, Madam! Just look!" She would say no; but he would tell her they were "Oh, so beautiful," and offer to give her some perfume, till perhaps if it were a dull afternoon she would roll up her knitting, and saunter down to the end of the hall where his dark little room was.

Since Mother had both a kind heart and a weakness for rugs, she was occasionally snared in this fashion and shown some bargain, some rug that was intrinsically priceless and could never be duplicated, but which could be had for a few hundred dollars, as it happened, that morning. The crisis that made such a price possible would tomorrow be gone, but today it was here, and a wise and clever woman would seize it. Whoever did would be helping a most grateful young man get through college. He was no dealer; he was just a poor student with a few priceless rugs, and if the lady would only make him an offer she could buy at her own figure. She could make him an offer, surely, *some* offer; let it be what it might.

It began to seem unreasonable to Mother not to make him some offer, especially as he was trying to get through college, and it might be a bargain. So she silently tried to figure how much she'd have had to pay at places like Sloane's; and then she took a lot off; and then she felt a little ashamed at taking so much off—she didn't wish to cheat the young man. He seemed to mean well, poor creature. So she worked her price up a little, in her mind, and then got a bit frightened because, after all, it was a good deal of money—though it did seem perfectly safe to pay that much, since Lord & Taylor's or Arnold Constable's would have charged more. Still, you never could tell about a rug, because it might not be genuine, and she wished the young man had let her alone and could get through college without her, though he didn't much look as though he would manage it; he could hardly speak English—and how could the poor thing talk to the professors, or the professors to him, when even on the subject of rugs he had to use a sort of sign language which consisted of hunching his shoulders till she feared he would dislocate them, and picking out sums on his fingers in the most confusing manner. However, she had better make him an offer, she felt, and then perhaps he'd stop smiling, which no doubt he intended as pleasant, but his breath was so bad.

So she finally said, fingering the rug in a dissatisfied way, that she supposed she could give him a hundred for it. The Armenian's smile instantly disappeared. He walked off in gloom. Then he rushed back, excited and jerky, and began a long, rapid expostulation that threatened to deafen us. Mother reluctantly raised her bid to a hundred and twenty to stop him, whereupon it suddenly appeared that he had misunderstood her first offer. He had supposed it to be two hundred, not one. She meant *two* hundred and twenty? Mother said, No, one hundred and twenty was all she had offered. The Armenian then tottered around, sank into a chair, and sort of hissed through his teeth, with such a ghastly look that it made Mother fear he might be having a fit. It began to seem advisable to her to do anything she could to get out of it, and then never buy anything again for the rest of her life. So she miserably and angrily said she would make it one-fifty. She had to say it several times, however, before he seemed to hear her, and even then he received it only with low shrieks and groans in Armenian. He said that now he would have to give up college, because he could not bear such losses. All he had ever hoped of America, he said, was that he wouldn't lose too much money here, but he had found that no one cared how badly he ruined himself, nor did they understand rugs. Poor Mother, half dismayed, half indignant, said she did not want the rug; she had only made him an offer because he had asked her to, and she would now like to go. This brought on a frightful collapse, so full of despair it seemed mortal. He was heard, however, to murmur what she took to be a dying request that she would take the rug with her and split the difference and leave him alone in his agony. On the way out, she had to tell the hotel-clerk to pay him and have it charged on the bill.

At the end of the week, when Father came to visit us and stay over Sunday, Mother had to explain to him that he was now the owner of a rare Eastern rug. Her attempts to announce this to him as a triumph somehow fell very flat. He began by not believing his ears, no matter how many times she repeated it. "Rug? Rug? You say you've bought a *rug*? Nonsense! Pooh! Don't be ridiculous!" And when he found that the story seemed true, and that he couldn't thrust it away, his face turned a dark unhealthy red and he burst into roars of resentment. He shouted that he had only just arrived from hard toil in the city, in search of "a little damned peace," that was all that he asked, instead of which, before he had had time to smoke one cigar, he was harried and tortured and victimized by a pack of low swindlers, with whom his own family had leagued themselves, to render him penniless. He urgently demanded to see the rug so that he could throw it straight out of the window, and the Armenian after it. He swore he'd break every bone in his body. All reports as to the rarity and value of the rug he discredited, declaring he could buy better for fifty cents a barrel on Front Street. He then marched to the Armenian's parlor, with vague but violent intentions, only to find that that astute sufferer had closed his place up. The door was shut and locked and a sign was on it:

B A K
N E K S
W E K

"What's this gibberish?" Father demanded. "You said his name was Dourbabian."

Poor old fawning Dourbabian! His things were not good value at the time; but they at least have become so. That rug and the sofa-cushion covers and great squares of silk which Mother picked up in the eighties would cost a lot more today. She had to keep them out of Father's sight though, until he had forgotten their origin.

Years afterwards, one day, when the newspapers printed some clergyman's denunciations of Turkey for its cruel Armenian massacres, I thought of how Father had longed to massacre Dourbabian, and reminded him of it. Though older and calmer on some subjects he was still resentful on this. "That's just like a parson," he said, "to sympathize with those fellows, without even asking first what they have done to the Turks."

CHAPTER 17

FATHER OPENS MY MAIL

THERE WAS a time in my boyhood when I felt that Father had handicapped me severely in life by naming me after him, "Clarence." All literature, so far as I could see, was thronged with objectionable persons named Clarence. Percy was bad enough, but there had been some good fighters named Percy. The only Clarence in history was a duke who did something dirty at Tewkesbury, and who died a ridiculous death afterwards in a barrel of malmsey.

As for the Clarences in the fiction I read, they were horrible. In one story, for instance, there were two brothers, Clarence and Frank. Clarence was a "vain, disagreeable little fellow," who was proud of his curly hair and fine clothes, while Frank was a "rollicking boy who was ready to play games with anybody." Clarence didn't like to play games, of course. He just minced around looking on.

One day when the mother of these boys had gone out, this story went on, Clarence "tempted" Frank to disobey her and fly their kite on the roof. Frank didn't want to, but Clarence kept taunting him and daring him until Frank was stung into doing it. After the two boys went up to the roof, Frank got good and dirty, running up and down and stumbling over scuttles, while Clarence sat there, giving him orders, and kept his natty clothes tidy. To my horror, he even spread out his handkerchief on the trapdoor to sit on. And to crown all, this sneak told on Frank as soon as their mother came in.

This wasn't an exceptionally mean Clarence, either. He was just run-of-the-mill. Some were worse.

So far as I could ever learn, however, Father had never heard of these stories, and had never dreamed of there being anything objectionable in his name. Quite the contrary. And yet as a boy he had lived a good rough-and-tumble boy's life. He had played and fought on the city streets, and kept a dog in Grandpa's stable, and stolen rides to Greenpoint Ferry on the high, lurching bus. In the summer he had gone to West Springfield and had run down Shad Lane through the trees to the house where Grandpa was born, and had gone barefoot and driven the cows home just as though he had been named Tom or Bill.

He had the same character as a boy, I suppose, that he had as a man, and he was too independent to care if people thought his name fancy. He paid no attention to the prejudices of others, except to disapprove of them. He had plenty of prejudices himself, of course, but they were his own. He was humorous and confident and level-headed, and I imagine that if any boy had tried to make fun of him for being named Clarence, Father would simply have laughed and told him he didn't know what he was talking about.

I asked Mother how this name had ever happened to spring up in our family. She explained that my great-great-grandfather was Benjamin Day, and my great-grandfather was Henry, and consequently my grandfather had been named Benjamin Henry. He in turn had named his eldest son Henry and his second son Benjamin. The result was that when Father was born there was no family name left. The privilege of choosing a name for Father had thereupon been given to Grandma, and unluckily for the Day family she had been reading a novel, the hero of which was named Clarence.

I knew that Grandma, though very like Grandpa in some respects, had a dreamy side which he hadn't, a side that she usually kept to

herself, in her serene, quiet way. Her romantic choice of this name
probably made Grandpa smile, but he was a detached sort of man
who didn't take small matters seriously, and who drew a good deal
of private amusement from the happenings of everyday life. Besides,
he was partly to blame in this case, because that novel was one he
had published himself in his magazine.

I asked Mother, when she had finished, why I had been named
Clarence too.

It hadn't been her choice, Mother said. She had suggested all
sorts of names to Father, but there seemed to be something wrong
with each one. When she had at last spoken of naming me after
him, however, he had said at once that that was the best suggestion
yet—he said it sounded just right.

Father and I would have had plenty of friction in any case. This
identity of names made things worse. Every time that I had been
more of a fool than he liked, Father would try to impress on me my
responsibilities as his eldest son, and above all as the son to whom
he had given his name, as he put it. A great deal was expected, it
seemed to me, of a boy who was named after his father. I used to
envy my brothers, who didn't have anything expected of them on
this score at all.

I envied them still more after I was old enough to begin getting
letters. I then discovered that when Father "gave" me his name he
had also, not unnaturally, I had to admit, retained it himself, and
when anything came for Clarence S. Day he opened it, though it
was sometimes for me.

He also opened everything that came addressed to Clarence S.
Day, Jr. He didn't do this intentionally, but unless the "Jr." was
clearly written, it looked like "Esq.," and anyhow Father was too
accustomed to open all Clarence Day letters to remember about
looking carefully every time for a "Jr." So far as mail and express
went, I had no name at all of my own.

For the most part nobody wrote to me when I was a small boy
except firms whose advertisements I had read in the *Youth's*

Companion and to whom I had written requesting them to send me their circulars. These circulars described remarkable bargains in magicians' card outfits, stamps and coins, pocket knives, trick spiders, and imitation fried eggs, and they seemed interesting and valuable to me when I got them. The trouble was that Father usually got them and at once tore them up. I then had to write for such circulars again, and if Father got the second one too, he would sometimes explode with annoyance. He became particularly indignant one year, I remembered, when he was repeatedly urged to take advantage of a special bargain sale of false whiskers. He said that he couldn't understand why these offerings kept pouring in. I knew why, in this case, but at other times I was often surprised myself at the number he got, not realizing that as a result of my postcard request my or our name had been automatically put on several large general mailing lists.

During this period I got more of my mail out of Father's wastebasket than I did from the postman.

At the age of twelve or thirteen, I stopped writing for these childish things and turned to a new field. Father and I, whichever of us got at the mail first, then began to receive not merely circulars but personal letters beginning:

DEAR FRIEND DAY:

In reply to your valued request for one of our Mammoth Agents' Outfits, kindly forward post-office order for $1.49 to cover cost of postage and packing, and we will put you in a position to earn a large income in your spare time with absolutely no labor on your part, by taking subscriptions for *The Secret Handbook of Mesmerism,* and our *Tales of Blood* series.

And one spring, I remember, as the result of what I had intended to be a secret application on my part, Father was assigned "the exclusive rights for Staten Island and Hoboken of selling the Gem Home Popper for Pop Corn. Housewives buy it at sight."

After Father had stormily endured these afflictions for a while, he and I began to get letters from girls. Fortunately for our feelings, these were rare, but they were ordeals for both of us. Father had forgotten, if he ever knew, how silly young girls can sound, and I got my first lesson in how unsystematic they were. No matter how private and playful they meant their letters to be, they forgot to put "Jr." on the envelope every once in so often. When Father opened these letters, he read them all the way through, sometimes twice, muttering to himself over and over: "This is very peculiar. I don't understand this at all. Here's a letter to me from some person I never heard of. I can't see what it's about." By the time it had occurred to him that possibly the letter might be for me, I was red and embarrassed and even angrier at the girl than at Father. And on days when he had read some of the phrases aloud to the family, it nearly killed me to claim it.

Lots of fellows whom I knew had been named after their fathers without having such troubles. But although Father couldn't have been kinder-hearted or had any better intentions, when he saw his name on a package or envelope it never dawned on him that it might not be for him. He was too active in his habits to wait until I had a chance to get at it. And as he was also single-minded and prompt to attend to unfinished business, he opened everything automatically and then did his best to dispose of it.

This went on even after I grew up, until I had a home of my own. Father was always perfectly decent about it, but he never changed. When he saw I felt sulky, he was genuinely sorry and said so, but he couldn't see why all this should annoy me, and he was surprised and amused that it did. I used to get angry once in a while when something came for me which I particularly hadn't wished him to see and which I would find lying, opened, on the hall table marked "For Jr.?" when I came in; but nobody could stay angry with Father—he was too utterly guiltless of having meant to offend.

He often got angry himself, but it was mostly at things, not at persons, and he didn't mind a bit (as a rule) when persons got angry at him. He even declared, when I got back from college, feeling dignified, and told him that I wished he'd be more careful, that he suffered from these mistakes more than I did. It wasn't *his* fault, he pointed out, if my stupid correspondents couldn't remember my name, and it wasn't any pleasure to him to be upset at his breakfast by finding that a damned lunatic company in Battle Creek had sent him a box of dry bread crumbs, with a letter asserting that this rubbish would be good for his stomach. "I admit I threw it into the fireplace, Clarence, but what else could I do? If you valued this preposterous concoction, my dear boy, I'm sorry. I'll buy another box for you today, if you'll tell me where I can get it. Don't feel badly! I'll buy you a barrel. Only I hope you won't eat it."

In the days when Mrs. Pankhurst and her friends were chaining themselves to lamp-posts in London, in their campaign for the vote, a letter came from Frances Hand trustfully asking "Dear Clarence" to do something to help Woman Suffrage—speak at a meeting, I think. Father got red in the face. "Speak at one of their meetings!" he roared at Mother. "I'd like nothing better! You can tell Mrs. Hand that it would give me great pleasure to inform all those crackpots in petticoats exactly what I think of their antics."

"Now, Clare," Mother said, "you mustn't talk that way. I like that nice Mrs. Hand, and anyhow this letter must be for Clarence."

One time I asked Father for his opinion of a low-priced stock I'd been watching. His opinion was that it was not worth a damn. I thought this over, but I still wished to buy it, so I placed a scale order with another firm instead of with Father's office, and said nothing about it. At the end of the month this other firm sent me a statement, setting forth each of my little transactions in full, and of course they forgot to put the "Jr." at the end of my name. When Father opened the envelope, he thought at first in his excitement that this firm had actually opened an account for him without being asked. I found him telling Mother that he'd like to wring their damned necks.

"That must be for me, Father," I said, when I took in what had happened.

We looked at each other.

"You bought this stuff?" he said incredulously. "After all I said about it?"

"Yes, Father."

He handed over the statement and walked out of the room.

Both he and I felt offended and angry. We stayed so for several days, too, but we then made it up.

Once in a while when I got a letter that I had no time to answer I used to address an envelope to the sender and then put anything in it that happened to be lying around on my desk—a circular about books, a piece of newspaper, an old laundry bill—anything at all, just to be amiable, and yet at the same time to save myself the trouble of writing. I happened to tell several people about this private habit of mine at a dinner one night—a dinner at which Alice Duer Miller and one or two other writers were present. A little later she wrote me a criticism of Henry James and ended by saying that I needn't send her any of my old laundry bills because she wouldn't stand it. And she forgot to put on the "Jr."

"In the name of God," Father said bleakly, "this is the worst yet. Here's a woman who says I'd better not read *The Golden Bowl,* which I have no intention whatever of doing, and she also warns me for some unknown reason not to send her my laundry bills."

The good part of all these experiences, as I realize now, was that in the end they drew Father and me closer together. My brother had only chance battles with him. I had a war. Neither he nor I relished its clashes, but they made us surprisingly intimate.

CHAPTER 18

FATHER SENDS ME TO
THE WORLD'S FAIR

FATHER AND Mother and my brothers went out to the World's Fair in Chicago in 1893. I was finishing my freshman year at Yale, and by the time I got home they had gone. Father had written me that I had better follow on and join them, but I couldn't. I had spent all my allowance. There would be no more money coming to me until college opened again in September. In the meantime I didn't even have carfare or money enough for tobacco. It wasn't this that bothered me, however, or not going out to Chicago. It was the fact that for the first time in my life I had got deep in debt.

I owed Warner Hall forty-two dollars for seven weeks' board, I owed Dole for a heavy turtleneck sweater, and De Bussy, Manwaring & Co. for ascot ties and shirts and a pair of pointed-toed shoes. I owed Heublein's for the rounds of drinks I had signed for, on what had once seemed jolly nights. I was in debt to Stoddard the tobacconist for sixty or seventy dollars for all sorts of fancy pipes—one of them was a meerschaum head of a bull with large amber horns. The total due to these and other tradesmen was nearly three hundred dollars, and I didn't see how I could have been so reckless, or when I could ever pay up. Worst of all, my creditors too had become pessimistic.

I borrowed a nickel for carfare from old Margaret, after she had cooked me my breakfast, put a sandwich and a banana in my pocket, and went downtown at once to Father's office to ask for a job. They didn't have any work for me down there and didn't want me around, but it was lucky I went, because while I was eating my sandwich one of my creditors entered. He had come down to New York with a bundle of overdue bills to see whether he could collect any of them by calling upon his customers' parents.

I was appalled. It had never occurred to me that anyone would come to Father's office like this. It seemed to me most underhanded. If Father had been there and I hadn't, I'd have been in serious trouble, for Father had warned me repeatedly to keep out of debt. I was thoroughly frightened, and I attempted to frighten that creditor. I said in a loud, shaky voice that if he was going to behave in this manner, I would never buy anything more from him as long as I lived.

He said he was sorry to hear it. But he didn't sound very sorry. Times were bad, he explained, and he had to have money. I didn't believe him. Looking back, I realize that the long depression of the nineties had started and banks were beginning to close, but I knew nothing about this at that time. I was preoccupied with my own troubles. These looked blacker than ever to me when my creditor said, as he left, that since my father was out, he would have to call on him again the next time he came to New York.

I didn't know what to do. But one thing was clear. I saw I must stick around Father's office for the rest of that summer. So as soon as he got back from the Fair, I begged him to give me a job. I didn't need any vacation, I told him, and I would be getting a lot of valuable experience if he would let me go to work.

After thinking it over, he said that perhaps I could make myself useful as an office boy while his clerks were taking turns going on their vacations. I started the very next day at four dollars a week.

I might have got slightly better wages elsewhere, but I couldn't have made enough anyway to pay much on my bills, and the most important thing was not to make a few dollars extra but to stand on guard at the door of Father's office to keep my creditors out. When I was sent out on an errand, I ran all the way there and back. When I was in the office, turning the big iron wheel on the letter press, I always kept one eye on the grated window where the cashier sat at his counter, to make sure that no old buzzards from New Haven were coming in to see Father.

But late in the summer I got into trouble. The cashier told Father that I had taken hold better than he had expected, and that although I was not very accurate I was punctual and quick and seemed to be especially interested in getting down early. Father was so pleased that he sent for me to come into his inner office and told me that he had decided I had earned a vacation.

I said that honestly and truly a vacation was the last thing I wanted.

He smiled at the immense pleasure I seemed to be taking in sealing envelopes and filling inkwells, but he explained that he wanted me to have some rest and recreation before college opened, and he added that he would advise me to go to Chicago and see the World's Fair.

I said I didn't care about seeing the Fair.

Father didn't quite like this. "I have just told you, Clarence," he said, "that I would advise you to go." I saw that he would regard it as disrespectful of me if I refused.

I uncomfortably made a partial confession. I said I couldn't afford to go to Chicago. I didn't have any money.

Father was surprised. "What about your allowance?" he asked.

"I'm sorry to say I've spent it all, Father."

"That was very imprudent of you," he observed.

I said in a low voice that I knew it.

Father said that he hoped this would be a lesson to me to be more careful in future. By failing to exercise even the most ordinary prudence, he explained in his firm, friendly way, I had deprived myself of seeing a sight that might never come again in my lifetime. He said he felt badly about it.

I didn't, however. I went back to working the letter press. I liked to turn the big, painted iron wheel and tighten the plates. We didn't use carbons. Instead, after writing letters by hand in copying ink or else on the typewriter, we pressed them down hard on damp tissue paper to make copies to file. It took a good deal of practice to do this correctly. If the tissue was too dry, the copy was so faint it could hardly be read, and if I got it too wet, it made the ink run and smudged the whole letter.

The next day, Father interrupted me at this interesting occupation again. He had had a long talk with Mother, it seemed, and, as all the rest of the family had seen the Fair, they wanted me to go, too. He said that he would therefore help me out this once and give me some money, and he asked how much I had saved from my wages.

I had saved nearly all of them, as a matter of fact. I had spent less than a dollar a week. Margaret had wrapped up little lunches for me, and my only other needs had been a haircut and carfares and a new pair of cuffs. But as I had been using all I saved to pay small installments to those men in New Haven, I had only forty-eight cents on hand.

"Well, the devil!" Father laughed disappointedly. "You have attended to your duties here faithfully enough, I suppose, but I see you have a damn lot to learn."

I thought to myself that he little knew how much I was learning.

He lit a cigar and looked at me reflectively. "Clarence," he said, "I think I should reproach myself afterward if I allowed you to miss seeing this Fair. It is a great educational opportunity that may never recur. So I will make you a present of one hundred dollars to enable you to go to Chicago."

"Thank you very much, Father," I said, as he shook hands with me, "but if you wouldn't mind, I'd rather have the money, sir."

Father frowned.

I stood beside his desk, waiting. A hundred dollars would be a magnificent windfall for me and my creditors.

His reply killed my hopes. "I see no point in giving you a hundred dollars to fritter away as you have done with your other funds," he said. "If you don't choose to avail yourself of this educational—"

"Oh, I do, sir," I said. If the only way to get that hundred dollars was to go to Chicago and back, I saw that of course I'd better go. I felt sure I could save at least some of it to use in paying my bills.

I went to the cashier and begged him to keep an eye out for my creditors and not let any of them in, in my absence. He said he would do all he could, but he wouldn't like to be caught surreptitiously keeping out callers. I argued that these people would annoy Father if they saw him, and that they ought to be treated like book-agents; but he said Father might regard their disclosures as important, however unwelcome, and that he couldn't keep anyone out who came on legitimate business.

I almost gave up going, at this. But Father and Mother were so eager to give me a treat that I couldn't. I had to pretend to be eager myself, with my heart in my boots.

I wrote to my creditors that I would begin paying my bills very soon and that I hoped they would wait.

Father asked me what road I was getting a ticket on. He said the Lake Shore was the best. I made some vague answer to that. I didn't like to tell him, after he had been so generous to me, that I had bought a cut-rate ticket to Chicago and back, for eleven dollars, on an Erie Special Excursion. The Erie was so awful in those days that it was a joke. It didn't go nearly as far as Chicago, of course, but it had arranged for trackage rights over a number of other one-horse railroads for its Special Excursions.

It took that train three days and two nights, if I remember correctly, to get to Chicago. We stopped at every small station. We waited for hours on sidings. Most of the time I had very little idea where we were. The Excursion wandered around here and there, in various parts of this country and Canada, trying to pick up extra passengers. Of course, the train had no sleeping cars or dinner—only day coaches. There was quite a crowd of us in them—men, women, and children. In the seat back of mine was a woman with two babies. I had my seat pretty much to myself, however, because the old man who sat with me spent most of his time in the smoker. I didn't go to the smoker myself. I had nothing to smoke.

All the windows were open, it was so hot. We were coated with coal dust. The washroom got out of order and had to be locked. The little drinking tank was soon emptied. Most of us had nothing to eat, and we slept sitting up. But it was fun. Nearly everybody but the overworked trainmen was good-natured and friendly. At every stop we'd all pile out of the cars and bolt for the washroom in the station, or try to buy pie and sandwiches and stand in line at the water-cooler, and those of us who went dry at one stop would try again at the next. At one little place where the station was locked and there was no other building in sight, we had the best luck of all, because there was a pond near the tracks, rather yellow, but with plenty of water for everybody. I was rinsing my undershirt in it when the whistle blew, and I only just managed to scramble aboard the train as it started. The day before that, at a little place where the eating was good, several passengers who didn't run fast enough had been left behind.

At Chicago, I hunted up a boarding house. As those near the Fair Grounds were expensive, I went to the outskirts, where I found an old boarding house near the railroad which was clean and decent. I sent off a postcard to Mother saying that the Fair was simply fine, and got a good bath and sleep.

I went to the Fair the next day. My boarding house was so far out that I had to go by train, but the fare was low and the station was handy. And when I walked into the Fair Grounds, I was deeply impressed. They were a wonderful sight. The vast buildings weren't solid stone, of course, and they wouldn't be there a hundred years hence, but in the meanwhile they provided a vision of grandeur, at least for innocent eyes. The eyes, for example, of persons who had come on the Erie.

I sat in the Court of Honor, I walked admiringly around the artificial lagoon, I sauntered through one or two of the exhibition halls, and went back to my boarding house.

On my next visit, I explored the grounds more thoroughly and I was upset to find that all the places which I wanted to see most cost money. This was particularly true of the Midway Plaisance, a broad promenade lined with sideshows. There were Bedouins, a Ferris Wheel, a fearsome (canvas) Hawaiian volcano, a wonderful captive balloon, and a "Congress of Beauty." And there was also a real Dahomey village of genuine savages. I could reach out and touch them as they stalked about, scowling; and whenever I did I could hear them muttering things to themselves. They occasionally danced in a threatening manner uttering genuine war-cries; and the guide-book said, "They also sell products of their mechanical skill." And, what had excited the most talk of all in the newspapers, there were dancing girls with bare stomachs, who wriggled in what clergymen said was a most abandoned way, right before everybody.

I had heard so much about these girls that I forgot all my vows to economize and went into their tent. They didn't come up to my hopes. I had already noticed in New Haven that such things never did.

That night in my boarding house, I counted my money, and I saw that if I had good times on the Midway, I'd have a bad time with creditors. My creditors won and I didn't go to the Midway again.

There was a great deal else to see, however, and I saw nearly all of it, because it was free. But as Father had said, it was educational. I spent hours and hours roaming through the principal exhibits which were supposed to be good for the mind. They were interesting but monotonous. It was like visiting a hundred museums at once. A few of these palaces fascinated me when I came to them fresh; the Krupp guns were better than anything on the Midway. But the showmanship wasn't. Herr Krupp had announced, by the way, that he was presenting the biggest gun of all to America, "for the defense of the great port of Chicago."

These free exhibits increased my expenses, some days; they made me so hungry. I had a hard time trying to be economical at the White Horse Inn, I remember. This was a reproduction of an old English inn, swollen to an extraordinary size, and the big chops at the next table looked juicy and the steaks smelled delicious. And every time I went to the Transportation Building and got in a coma, I had to revive myself on beer and cheese afterward in a place called Old Vienna.

Father had especially enjoined upon me the duty of studying the Transportation Exhibits, because he was an officer or director of several small railroads, and he hoped that by and by I might be too. It was quite an assignment. That building had eighteen acres of floor-space. It was built in the form of several large train sheds. The guide-book explained that "in style it is somewhat Romanesque," and it added that "the ornamental color designs, in thirty different shades, of its exterior, produce an effect almost as fine as embroidery."

On rainy days I didn't go to the Fair Grounds. I sat in my boarding house and saved money. But this was dull and I felt lonely, so I bought a chameleon for company. He wasn't much company. On the other hand, as the end of his tail had been broken off, he only cost twenty cents. He wore a chain with a little brass collar at one end and a pin at the other, and I stuck the pin in the window curtain to tether him, and fed him live flies.

I wanted to go home after a week of this, but I figured that I'd better not. Father might think I had been too lavish with his money if it only lasted a week. So I stayed on for over a fortnight to inspire him with confidence in me, and make him see that I wasn't always a spendthrift in spite of my bad freshman record.

When I wasn't at the Fair, I wandered around Chicago. There was something about Chicago I liked. It seemed bigger and busier to me than New York, and much fatter, much more spread-out and roomy.

At last, when I thought Father must surely be feeling that I had used up that hundred dollars, I packed my suitcase, pinned the chameleon to the lapel of my coat, and embarked again on the Erie. The chameleon had a miserable time on the train and the rest of his tail got joggled off, but even so he was luckier than he knew, for we made much better time going east than we had made going west.

I had gone away worried and alarmed, but I came home in triumph. No creditors had gone to the office, I learned, and I had saved fifty-two dollars to send to New Haven. I hadn't brought home any presents for the family, but I presented the chameleon to Mother.

Father and I had a little talk about what I had liked. "Did you see the Midway?" he asked.

"I saw a little of it," I said cautiously. "Did you see it, Father?"

"Yes," he said, "I was interested in those filthy Hottentots. How people can live in that disgusting manner I don't understand. I didn't know it was allowed."

He was pleased when he found I had gone only once to the Midway and had apparently spent all the rest of my time in the right places.

"Well," he finally said in approval, "I gather, then, that you found it was an educational experience for you."

"Yes, Father," I told him, "I did."

CHAPTER 19

FATHER'S OLD TROUSERS

FATHER DIDN'T care much for jewelry. He disliked the heavy watch-chains which were worn by the men of his time, chains with charms dangling down from the middle. His had none of these things on it; it was strong and handsome but simple. His studs and cuff-links were on the same order, not ornate like those then in fashion. His ring was a solid plain band of gold, set with a rectangular sapphire. All these objects we regarded with a reverence which we felt was their due. There was a special sort of rightness about Father's things, in our eyes, and we had a special respect for them because they were Father's.

Father had had a lighter ring once, with a smaller sapphire, which he had worn as a young man. He had discarded it as less suitable for him, however, as he got on in life, and it had been put away long ago in the safe in our pantry.

Mother didn't like to have it lying idle there, year after year. After I left college, she decided that I had better wear it, so that the family would get some good out of it once more. One afternoon she and I went into the crowded pantry, with its smell of damp washcloths, and she took it out of the safe.

I did not want a ring, but Mother presented this one to me with such affection that I saw no way to get out of accepting it. She put it on my finger and kissed me. I looked at the thing. The sapphire was a beautiful little stone. I thought that after a while I might learn to like it, perhaps. At any rate, there was nothing to get out of order or break.

I soon discovered, however, that this ring was a nuisance—it was such hard work not to lose it. If I had bought and paid for it myself, I suppose I'd have cherished it, but as it had been wished on me, it was only a responsibility. It preyed on my mind. After a little while, I stopped wearing it and put it away.

When Mother noticed that it wasn't on my finger, she spoke out at once. She said there wasn't much point in my having a ring if I merely kept it in my bureau drawer. She reminded me that it was a very handsome ring and I ought to be proud to wear it.

I explained that I couldn't get used to remembering that I was wearing a ring, and had several times left it on public washstands and got it back only by sheer luck. Mother was frightened. She instantly agreed that it would be a terrible thing to lose Father's ring. It went back into the safe in the pantry.

Several years later, it was taken out again, and after another little ceremony it was entrusted to George. He had even more trouble with it than I'd had. He, too, decided that he didn't wish to wear it himself, so, as he had married, he gave it to his wife, who adored it. Everyone was happy for a while until Mother happened to see Father's ring nestling on Wilhelmine's finger. Mother was very fond of Wilhelmine, but this strange sight disturbed her. She felt that the only right and appropriate use for that ring was for it to be worn by one of Father's sons. She asked George to take it away from Wilhelmine and return it. He silently did so, and back it went again to the pantry.

It was a curious fact that everything that Father had ever owned seemed to be permanently a part of him. No matter what happened to it, it remained impressed with his personality. This isn't unusual

in the case of a ring, I suppose, but the same thing was true even of
Father's old neckties, especially from his point of view. I don't think
he cared what became of that ring, the way Mother did, but when
he gave me an old necktie or a discarded pair of trousers, they still
seemed to him to be his. Not only did he feel that way about it but
he made me feel that way, too. He explained to me that he gave
things which he didn't care about to the coachman or the Salvation
Army, but that when he had a particularly handsome tie which had
plenty of wear in it yet, or a pair of trousers which he had been fond
of, he saved anything of that sort for me.

A pair of striped trousers which he had worn to church on
Sundays for years went up to New Haven with me one Chirstmas,
when I was a junior, and as I was short of clothes at the time, they
came in very handy. I had to be careful not to take off my coat while
I was wearing them, though. They looked oddly baggy in the seat
when exposed to full view—on nights when I was playing billiards
in a poolroom, for instance. They also made it harder for me to
climb Osborn Hall's iron gate. This gate was ten feet high, with a
row of long, sharp spikes at the top, and to get quickly over it in
Father's trousers was quite a feat.

There was no point in getting over it quickly. In fact, there was
no point in getting over it at all. Osborn Hall was used solely for
lectures, and we saw quite enough of it in the daytime without trying to get in there at night. Besides, we couldn't get in anyhow, even
after climbing the gate because the big inside doors were locked fast.
After standing in the vestibule a minute, between the doors and the
gate, there was nothing to do but climb back again and go home to
bed. This seemed like a useful or stimulating performance, though,
when we had been drinking.

On nights like these, as I was undressing in my bedroom, I sometimes had moral qualms over the way that I was making Father's
trousers lead this new kind of life. Once in a while such misgivings
would even come over me elsewhere. They were not clear-cut or
acute, but they floated around in the back of my mind. Usually I

paid little attention to what clothes I had on, but when I did happen to notice that I was wearing those trousers into places which were not respectable, I didn't feel right about it.

Then one week I lent them to a classmate of mine, Jerry Ives, to wear in his role of a fat man in some Psi U play. Father wasn't fat, but he was much more full-bodied than Jerry, and there was plenty of room in his trousers for a pillow and Jerry besides. I thought no more of the matter until the night of the play, but when the curtain went up and I saw Father's Sunday trousers running across the stage pursued by a comic bartender who was yelling "Stop thief!" I felt distinctly uncomfortable.

After that, nothing seemed to go right with them. The fact was, they simply didn't fit into undergraduate life. The night that I most fully realized this, I remember, was when a girl whom Father would have by no means approved of sat on what was my lap but his trousers. Father was a good eighty miles away and safely in bed, but I became so preoccupied and ill at ease that I got up and left.

CHAPTER 20

FATHER LETS IN THE TELEPHONE

UP TO the late eighteen-nineties, when Father walked in the front door of his home and closed it behind him, he shut out the world. Telephones had been invented but, like most people, he hadn't installed one. There was no way for anybody to get at us except by climbing up the front stoop and ringing the bell; and if the bell rang late at night, Father looked out of the window to see who it was. He thought nothing of this—homes had always been shut off since men began building them, and it seemed only natural.

Once in a long while a messenger boy would bring him or Mother a telegram—maybe two or three times a year. As this generally meant bad news, we were nervous about getting telegrams.

No telegraph poles were allowed on Fifth Avenue, but they stood in long rows on other thoroughfares. Old Margaret was mystified by all those wires, up in the air. We had wires in our house, to be sure; they had been strung inside the walls to ring bells with; but they were good, honest, old-fashioned wires and to make them work we had to pull them. There was none of this dangerous stuff called electricity in them. Electricity was much too risky a thing to put in a home, and neither we boys nor Margaret could make out what it was. All we knew about it was that there were electric batteries in the Eden Musée which could and did give anyone who paid twenty-five cents a shock. You were supposed to give yourself as big a shock as you could stand. We had been cautious in trying them, except George, who had had a startling experience. He had taken hold of one end of the thing in his right hand and moved it way up, till the indicator pointed to far more "current" than the rest of us had been able to stand, and yet he stood there at ease for a while as though he were completely immune. Then the lady in charge noticed that George hadn't taken the other end in his left hand at all. He hadn't understood that he ought to. When she told him that the way to feel the current was to hold one end in each hand, he immediately seized the left hand one without lowering the right from its height. It was grandly exciting to the rest of us to see how violently this shook him up, and how the lady screamed until attendants rushed over and managed to shut off the current.

After a while the telegraph company persuaded Father to let them install a brand new invention, just inside of one of our back bedroom windows, where it couldn't do any harm. This was a small metal box with a handle. A wire led from it which was connected with a telegraph pole, but although there was some electricity in it there was only a little, and the company guaranteed it was safe. The handle was made to look just those on the pull-bells which we were used to. When we pulled it, the box began to buzz, and somehow that sent a signal to the nearest telegraph office, where a row of little messenger boys was supposed to be waiting. The office then sent a boy to our house ready to run any errand.

This "buzzer," as we called it, seemed almost as remarkable to us as that lamp of Aladdin's. By giving some extra pulls on it and making it buzz enough times, the directions said, a policeman could be summoned, or even a fire engine.

How long it would have taken for a policeman to come we never
had occasion to learn. It took a messenger boy from twenty to forty-
five minutes—that is, if we were lucky. The branch office was nearly
a mile away and it had only one little benchful of boys. If the boys
were all out when we buzzed for one, the manager had no way to
tell us. We might be impatient. He wasn't. He peacefully waited till
some boy got through other errands.

On stormy days sometimes, when a friend wished to send us a
message or break an engagement, a messenger would surprise us by
coming without being buzzed for. He stood outside the front door,
with a black rubber hood dripping with rain hanging down from
his cap, blowing on his cold fingers and stamping, and ringing away
at the bell. And when one of us opened the door, the boy would
thrust in a wet letter and hoarsely ask us to sign the name and the
hour on a small, smudgy slip.

All these delays were more or less put up with, however. There
was no other service to turn to. And anyway people seldom used
messengers—they were not only slow but expensive. We ran our
own errands.

When the telephone was invented and was ready to use, hardly
anybody cared to install one. We all stuck to our buzzers. Messenger boys were quite enough of a nuisance, suddenly appearing at
the door with a letter and expecting an answer. But they came only
a few times a year, and a telephone might ring every week. People
admitted that telephones were ingenious contraptions and wondered just how they worked, but they no more thought of getting
one than of buying a balloon or a diving suit.

As a matter of fact, for a long time they were of little use in a
home. Since almost nobody had them but brokers, there was no
one to talk to. The telephone company sent us circulars in which
they made large claims: they said that an important department
store now had a telephone, and three banks had ordered one apiece,
and some enterprising doctors were getting them. But though people saw vaguely that a telephone might be a convenience if every

household installed one, they decided to wait in a body until everyone did.

Father had to have one downtown, but he wouldn't use it himself; he had it put in the back office, where the bookkeeper dealt with it, bringing Father the message if necessary. The typewriter and a gelatine hektograph were in the back office, too. But the idea of putting these business conveniences in a home seemed absurd.

Mother agreed with Father—she didn't like telephones either. She distrusted machines of all kinds; they weren't human, they popped or exploded and made her nervous. She never knew what they might do to her. And the telephone seemed to her, and many other people, especially dangerous. They were afraid that if they stood near one in a thunderstorm they might get hit by lightning. Even if there wasn't any storm, the electric wiring might give them a shock. When they saw a telephone in some hotel or office, they stood away from it or picked it up gingerly. It was a freak way to use electricity, and Mother wouldn't even touch the queer toy. Besides, she said, she had to see the face of any person she talked to. She didn't want to be answered by a voice coming out of a box on the wall.

Little by little, however, and year by year, telephones came into use. Some of the large markets and groceries installed them. The livery stable. Some druggists. And once in a while, when Father had a bad cold and couldn't go to the office, he saw it would be a business convenience to have one at home.

After ten or fifteen years, in spite of his still having misgivings, he got one. It was put on a wall on the second floor, where everybody could hear its loud bell. We didn't give it much of a welcome. It seemed to us rude and intrusive, and from the first it made trouble. It rang seldom but it always chose a bad moment, when there was nobody on that floor to answer. Mother would pick up her skirts and run upstairs, calling to it loudly "I'm coming! I'm coming!" but the fretful thing kept right on ringing. Father couldn't regard it as inanimate either. He refused to be hurried like Mother, but he scolded and cursed it.

The outer world now began intruding upon us at will. This was hard to get used to. Even Mother felt there was too much of it. As for Father, he met these invasions with ferocious resentment. When somebody telephoned him and he couldn't make out at once who it was, and when there was nothing he could shake his fist at but a little black receiver which was squeaking at him, he said it was horrible. "Speak up, speak up, damn it!" he would shout at the telephone, getting red in the face. "What is it, who are you? I can't hear a word you are saying. I can't hear a damned word, I tell you."

"Clare, give me that telephone!" Mother would cry, rushing in.

"I will not give you this telephone!" Father would roar in reply, without taking his lips from the transmitter. "Will you let me alone? I am trying to find out who the devil this person is. Halloa! I say halloa there, do you hear me? Who are you? Halloa! . . . What's that? . . . Oh, it's you, Mrs. Nichols." Here his voice would grow a little less forbidding, and sometimes even friendly. "Yes, Mrs. Day's here. How are you? . . . Oh, do you wish to speak to Mrs. Day? . . . Eh? . . . Very well then. Wait a moment." And he would at last allow Mother to get at the box on the wall.

When Father called a number himself, he usually got angry at "Central." He said she was deaf, she was stupid, he told her she wasn't attending to her duties in a suitable manner. If she said a number was busy, he'd protest: "I can't sit here waiting all day. Busy? Busy be damned!"

He always assumed when the bell rang that it was a message for him. The idea that it might be a call for Mother or one of the rest of us seemed wholly improbable. If he let anyone but himself answer, he would keep calling out and asking who it was and what it was all about anyhow, while we tried, in the midst of his shouts, to hear some of the message. When we said it was something that didn't concern him, he was incredulous, and had to have it explained to make sure.

One day a new friend of mine, a girl who had moved down to live in a settlement house in the slums, telephoned to invite me to lunch with some visiting Russians. Father answered the telephone. "Yes, this is Mr. Day. Speak up, hang it! Don't mumble at me. Who are you? . . . *What?* Come to lunch? I've had lunch. . . . Next Friday? Why, I don't want to lunch with you next Friday. . . . No. . . . Where? Where do you say? . . . In Rivington Street? The devil! . . . Yes, my name is Clarence Day and I told you that before. Don't repeat. . . . Lunch with you in Rivington Street? Good God! I never heard of such a thing in my life! . . . Russians? I don't know any Russians. . . . No, I don't want to, either. . . . No, I haven't changed. I never change. . . . What? . . . Goodbye, Madam. Damn!"

"I think that was a friend of mine, Father," I said.

"A friend of yours!" he exclaimed. "Why, it sounded to me like some impudent peddler's wife this time, arguing with me about lunching with her somewhere down in the slums. I can't stand it, that's all I have to say. I'll have the confounded thing taken out."

CHAPTER 21

FATHER ISN'T MUCH HELP

IN FATHER'S childhood it was unusual for boys to take music lessons, and his father hadn't had him taught music. Men didn't play the piano. Young ladies learned to play pretty things on it as an accomplishment, but few of them went further, and any desire to play classical music was rare.

After Father grew up, however, and began to do well in his business, he decided that music was one of the good things of life. He bought himself a piano and paid a musician to teach him. He took no interest in the languishing love songs which were popular then, he didn't admire patriotic things such as "Marching Through Georgia," and he had a hearty distaste for songs of pathos—he always swore if he heard them. He enjoyed music as he did a fine wine or a good ride on horseback.

The people he associated with didn't care much for this kind of thing, and Father didn't wish to associate with the long-haired musicians who did. He got no encouragement from anyone and his progress was lonely. But Father was not the kind of man who depends on encouragement. He had long muscular fingers, he practiced faithfully, and he learned to the best of his ability to play Beethoven and Bach.

His feeling for music was limited but it was deeply rooted, and he cared enough for it to keep on practicing even after he married and in the busy years when he was providing for a house full of boys. He didn't go to symphonic concerts and he never liked Wagner, but he'd hum something of Brahms while posting his ledger, or play Mozart or Chopin after dinner. It gave him a sense of well-being.

Mother liked music too. We often heard her sweet voice gently singing old songs of an evening. If she forgot parts here or there, she swiftly improvised something that would let the air flow along without breaking the spell.

Father didn't play that way. He was erecting much statelier structures, and when he got a chord wrong, he stopped. He took that chord apart and went over the notes one by one, and he kept on going over them methodically. This sometimes drove Mother mad. She would desperately cry "Oh-oh-oh!" and run out of the room.

Her whole attitude toward music was different. She didn't get a solid and purely personal enjoyment from it like Father. It was more of a social function to her. It went with dancing and singing. She played and sang for fun, or to keep from being sad, or to give others pleasure.

On Thursday afternoons in the winter, Mother was always "at home." She served tea and cakes, and quite a few people dropped in to see her. She liked entertaining. And whenever she saw a way to make her Thursdays more attractive, she tried it.

About this time, Mother's favorite niece, Cousin Julie, was duly "finished" at boarding school and came to live with us, bringing her trunks and hatboxes and a great gilded harp. Mother at once made room for this beautiful object in our crowded parlor, and the first thing Julie knew she had to play it for the Thursday-afternoon visitors. Julie loved her harp dearly but she didn't like performing at all—performances frightened her, and if she fumbled a bit, she felt badly. But Mother said she must get over all that. She tried to give Julie self-confidence. She talked to her like a determined though kind impresario.

These afternoon sessions were pleasant, but they made Mother want to do more. While she was thinking one evening about what a lot of social debts she must pay, she suddenly said to Father, who was reading Gibbon, half-asleep by the fire, "Why not give a musicale, Clare, instead of a series of dinners?"

When Father was able to understand what she was talking about, he said he was glad if she had come to her senses sufficiently to give up any wild idea of having a series of dinners, and that she had better by all means give up musicales, too. He informed her he was not made of money, and all good string quartets were expensive; and when Mother interrupted him, he raised his voice and said, to close the discussion: "I will not have my peaceful home turned into a Roman arena, with a lot of hairy fiddlers prancing about and disturbing my comfort."

"You needn't get so excited, Clare," Mother said. "I didn't say a word about hairy fiddlers. I don't know where you get such ideas. But I do know a lovely young girl whom Mrs. Spiller has had, and she'll come for very little, I'm sure."

"What instrument does this inexpensive paragon play?" Father inquired sardonically.

"She doesn't play, Clare. She whistles."

"Whistles!" said Father. "Good God!"

"Very well, then," Mother said after an argument. "I'll have to have Julie instead, and Miss Kregman can help her, and I'll try to get Sally Brown or somebody to play the piano."

"Miss Kregman!" Father snorted. "I wash my hands of the whole business."

Mother asked nothing better. She could have made a grander affair of it if he had provided the money, but even with only a little to spend, getting up a party was fun. Before her marriage, she had loved her brother Alden's musicales. She would model hers upon those. Hers would be different in one way, for Uncle Alden had had famous artists, and at hers the famous artists would be impersonated by Cousin Julie. But the question as to how expert the music would be didn't bother her, and she didn't think it would bother the guests whom she planned to invite. The flowers would be pretty; she knew just what she would put in each vase (the parlor was full of large vases); she had a special kind of little cakes in mind, and everybody would enjoy it all thoroughly.

But no matter what kind of artists she has, a hostess is bound to have trouble managing them, and Mother knew that even her homemade material would need a firm hand. Julie was devoted to her, and so was the other victim, Sally Brown, Julie's schoolmate. But devoted or not, they were uneasy about this experiment. Sally would rather have done almost anything than perform at a musicale, and the idea of playing in public sent cold chills down Julie's back.

The only one Mother worried about, however, was Julie's teacher, Miss Kregman. She could bring a harp of her own, so she would be quite an addition, but Mother didn't feel she was decorative. She was an angular, plain-looking woman, and she certainly was a very unromantic sight at a harp.

Father didn't feel she was decorative either, and said, "I'll be hanged if I come." He said musicales were all poppycock anyway. "Nothing but tinkle and twitter."

"Nobody's invited you, Clare," Mother said defiantly. As a matter of fact, she felt relieved by his announcement. This wasn't like a dinner, where she wanted Father and where he would be of some use. She didn't want him at all at her musicale.

"All I ask is," she went on, "that you will please dine out for once. It won't be over until six at the earliest, and it would make things much easier for me if you would dine at the club."

Father said that was ridiculous. "I never dine at the club. I won't do it. Any time I can't have my dinner in my own home, this house is for sale. I disapprove entirely of these parties and uproar!" he shouted. "I'm ready to sell the place this very minute if I can't live here in peace, and we can all go and sit under a palm tree and live on breadfruit and pickles!"

On the day of the musicale, it began to snow while we were at breakfast. Father had forgotten what day it was, of course, and he didn't care anyhow—his mind was on a waistcoat which he wished Mother to take to his tailor's. To his astonishment, he found her standing on a stepladder, arranging some ivy, and when he said "Here's my waistcoat," she gave a loud wail of self-pity at this new infliction. Father said in a bothered way: "What is the matter with you, Vinnie? What are you doing up on that ladder? Here's my waistcoat, I tell you, and it's got to go to the tailor at once." He insisted on handing it up to her, and he banged the front door going out.

Early in the afternoon, the snow changed to rain. The streets were deep in slush. We boys gave up sliding downhill on the railroad bridge in East Forty-eighth Street and came tramping in with our sleds. Before going up to the playroom, we looked in the parlor. It was full of small folding chairs. The big teakwood armchairs with their embroidered backs were crowded off into corners, and the blue velvety ottoman with its flowered top could hardly be seen. The rubber tree had been moved from the window and strategically placed by Miss Kregman's harp, in such a way that the harp would be in full view but Miss Kregman would not.

Going upstairs, we met Julie coming down. Her lips were blue. She was pale. She passed us with fixed, unseeing eyes, and when I touched her hand it felt cold.

Looking over the banisters, we saw Miss Kregman arrive in her galoshes. Sally Brown, who was usually gay, entered silently later. Miss Kregman clambered in behind the rubber tree and tuned the majestic gold harps. Mother was arranging trayfuls of little cakes and sandwiches, and giving a last touch to the flowers. Her excited voice floated up to us. There was not a sound from the others.

At the hour appointed for this human sacrifice, ladies began arriving in long, swishy dresses which swept bits of mud over the carpet. Soon the parlor was packed. I thought of Sally, so anxious and numb she could hardly feel the piano keys, and of Julie's icy fingers plucking valiantly away at the strings. Then Mother clapped her hands as a signal for the chatter to halt, the first hesitating strains of music began, and someone slid the doors shut.

When we boys went down to dinner that evening, we heard the news, good and bad. In a way it had been a success. Julie and Sally had played beautifully the whole afternoon, and the ladies had admired the harps, and applauded, and eaten up all the cakes. But there had been two catastrophes. One was that although Miss Kregman herself had been invisible, everybody had kept looking fascinatedly at her feet, which had stuck out from the rubber tree, working away by themselves, as it were, at the pedals, and the awful part was she had forgotten to take off her galoshes. The other was that Father had come home during a sweet little lullaby and the ladies had distinctly heard him say "Damn" as he went up to his room.

CHAPTER 22

FATHER SEWS ON A
BUTTON

IT MUST have been hard work to keep up with the mending in our house. Four boys had to be kept in repair besides Father, and there was no special person to do it. The baby's nurse did some sewing, and Cousin Julie turned to and did a lot when she was around, but the rest of it kept Mother busy and her work basket was always piled high.

Looking back, I wonder now how she managed it. I remember her regularly going off to her room and sewing on something, right after dinner or at other idle moments, when she might have sat around with the rest of us. My impression as a boy was that this was like going off to do puzzles—it was a form of amusement, or a woman's way of passing the time.

There was more talk about Father's socks and shirts than anything else. Most of this talk was by Father, who didn't like things to disappear for long periods, and who wanted them brought promptly back and put in his bureau drawer where they belonged. This was particularly true of his favorite socks. Not the plain white ones which he wore in the evening, because they were all alike, but the colored socks that were supplied to him by an English haber-dasher in Paris.

These colored socks were the one outlet of something in Father which ran contrary to that religion of propriety to which he adhered. In that day of somber hues for men's suits and quiet tones for men's neckties, most socks were as dark and severe as the rest of one's gar-ments; but Father's, hidden from the public eye by his trousers and his high buttoned shoes, had a really astonishing range both of color and fancy. They were mostly in excellent taste, but in a distinctly French way, and Wilhelmine used to tease him about them. She called them his "secret joys."

Father got holes in his socks even oftener than we boys did in our stockings. He had long athletic toes, and when he lay stretched out on his sofa reading and smoking, or absorbed in talking to any-one, these toes would begin stretching and wiggling in a curious way by themselves, as though they were seizing on this chance to live a life of their own. I often stared in fascination at their leisurely twistings and turnings, when I should have been listening to Father's instructions about far different matters. Soon one and then the other slipper would fall off, always to Father's surprise, but without inter-rupting his talk, and a little later his busy great toe would peer out at me through a new hole in his sock.

Mother felt that it was a woman's duty to mend things and sew, but she hated it. She rather liked to embroider silk lambrequins, as a feat of womanly prowess, but her darning of Father's socks was an impatient and not-too-skillful performance. She said there were so many of them that they made the back of her neck ache.

Father's heavily starched shirts, too, were a problem. When he put one on, he pulled it down over his head, and thrust his arms blindly out right and left in a hunt for the sleeves. A new shirt was strong enough to survive these strains without splitting, but life with Father rapidly weakened it, and the first thing he knew he would hear it beginning to tear. That disgusted him. He hated any evidence of weakness, either in people or things. In his wrath he would strike out harder than ever as he felt around for the sleeve. Then would come a sharp crackling noise as the shirt ripped open, and a loud wail from Mother.

Buttons were Father's worst trial, however, from his point of view. Ripped shirts and socks with holes in them could still be worn, but drawers with their buttons off couldn't. The speed with which he dressed seemed to discourage his buttons and make them desert Father's service. Furthermore, they always gave out suddenly and at the wrong moment.

He wanted help and he wanted it promptly at such times, of course. He would appear at Mother's door with a waistcoat in one hand and a disloyal button in the other, demanding that it be sewn on at once. If she said she couldn't just then, Father would get as indignant as though he had been drowning and a life-guard had informed him he would save him tomorrow.

When his indignation mounted high enough to sweep aside his good judgment, he would say in a stern voice, "Very well, I'll sew it on myself," and demand a needle and thread. This announcement always caused consternation. Mother knew only too well what it meant. She would beg him to leave his waistcoat in her work basket and let her do it next day. Father was inflexible. Moreover, his decision would be strengthened if he happened to glance at her basket and see how many of his socks were dismally waiting there in that crowded exile.

"I've been looking for those blue polka-dotted socks for a month," he said angrily one night before dinner. "Not a thing is done for a man in this house. I even have to sew on my own buttons. Where is your needle and thread?"

Mother reluctantly gave these implements to him. He marched off, set on the edge of his sofa in the middle of his bedroom, and got ready to work. The gaslight was better by his bureau, but he couldn't sit on a chair when he sewed. It had no extra room on it. He laid his scissors, the spool of thread, and his waistcoat down on the sofa beside him, wet his fingers, held the needle high up and well out in front, and began poking the thread at the eye.

Like every commander, Father expected instant obedience, and he wished to deal with trained troops. The contrariness of the needle and the limp obstinacy of the thread made him swear. He stuck the needle in the sofa while he wet his fingers and stiffened the thread again. When he came to take up his needle, it had disappeared. He felt around everywhere for it. He got up, holding fast to his thread, and turned around, facing the sofa to see where it was hiding. This jerked the spool off onto the floor, where it rolled away and unwound.

The husbands of two of Mother's friends had had fits of apoplexy and died. It frightened her horribly when this seemed about to happen to Father. At the sound of his roars, she rushed in. There he was on the floor, as she had feared. He was trying to get his head under the sofa and he was yelling at something, and his face was such a dark red and his eyes so bloodshot that Mother was terrified. Pleading with him to stop only made him more apoplectic. He said he'd be damned if he'd stop. He stood up presently, tousled but triumphant, the spool in his hand. Mother ran to get a new needle. She threaded it for him and he at last started sewing.

Father sewed on the button in a violent manner, with vicious haulings and jabs. Mother said she couldn't bear to see him—but she couldn't bear to leave the room, either. She stood watching him, hypnotized and appalled, itching to sew it herself, and they talked at each other with vehemence. Then the inevitable accident happened: the needle came forcibly up through the waistcoat, it struck on the button, Father pushed at it harder, and it burst through the hole and stuck Father's finger.

He sprang up with a howl. To be impaled in this way was not only exasperating, it was an affront. He turned to me, as he strode about on the rug, holding onto his finger, and said wrathfully, "It was your mother."

"Why Clare!" Mother cried.

"Talking every minute," Father shouted at her, "and distracting a man! How the devil can I sew on a button with this gibbering and buzz in my ears? Now see what you made me do!" he added suddenly. "Blood on my good waistcoat! Here! Take the damned thing. Give me a handkerchief to tie up my finger with. Where's the witch-hazel?"

CHAPTER 23

FATHER AND THE CRUSADER'S THIRD WIFE

ONE OF the ways in which Father and Mother were as alike as two peas was in their love of having good times. When they went to a dance or a dinner where they enjoyed themselves, they were full of high spirits. They had a lot of gusto about it, and they came home refreshed.

But there was this great difference: Mother always wanted to go; Father never. Mother was eager, and she was sure in advance they would like it. She had a romantic idea, Father said, that all parties were pleasant. He knew better. He said he hated them. All of them. He refused to go anywhere. When Mother asked him about accepting this or that invitation, he said she could go if she liked, but he certainly wouldn't. He would settle down in his chair and say, "Thank God, *I* know enough to stay home."

But Mother couldn't go to a dance or a dinner without him. That would have been impossible in those days. It was almost unheard of. The result was that she accepted all invitations and didn't tell him until the time came to go, so that Father went out much more than he meant to; only he always made a scene first, of course, and had to be dragged.

Every time he got into the carriage and drove off to their friends', he felt imposed upon and indignant, and Mother was almost worn out.

The surprising thing was that after all this, both of them had a good time. They both had immense stores of energy and resilience to draw on. Mother would alight from the carriage half-crying, but determined to enjoy herself, too; and Father, who could never stay cross for long, would begin to cheer up as soon as he went in the big, lighted doorway. By the time they were at table or in the ballroom, they were both full of fun.

"Aren't you ashamed of yourself," she would say, "making such a fuss about coming!"

But Father had forgotten the fuss by then, and would ask what on earth she was talking about.

When he sat next to some pretty woman at table, his eye would light up and he would feel interested and gallant. He had charm. Women liked him. It never did them any good to like him if the wine wasn't good, or if the principal dishes weren't cooked well. That made him morose. But when the host knew his business, Father was gay and expansive, without ever a thought of the raps Mother would give him on the head going home.

"Clare, you were so silly with that Miss Remsen! She was laughing at you all the time."

"What are you talking about now?" he would chuckle, trying to remember which was Miss Remsen. He was not good at names, and pretty women were much the same to him anyhow. He was attentive and courtly to them by instinct, and Mother could see they felt flattered, but no one would have been as startled as Father if this had made complications. He thought of his marriage as one of those things that were settled. If any woman had really tried to capture him, she would have had a hard time. He was fully occupied with his business and his friends at the club, and he was so completely wrapped up in Mother that she was the one his eye followed. He liked to have a pretty woman next to him, as he liked a cigar or a flower, but if either a flower or a cigar had made demands on him, he would have been most disturbed.

It thrilled Mother, at parties, to meet some distinguished and proud-looking man, especially if he made himself agreeable to her, for she greatly admired fine males. She was critical too, though; they had to be human to please her. She was swift at pricking balloons. If there were no one of this high type to fascinate her, she liked men who were jolly; quick-minded men who danced well or talked well. Only they mustn't make love to her. When they did, she was disappointed in them. She said they were idiots. She not only said so to others, she said so to them. "Mercy on us, Johnny Baker," she'd say crossly, "don't be such a fool!"

Johnny Baker belonged to his wife, that was Mother's idea, and if he didn't know it, he was stupid. Mother hated stupidity. She seemed to go on the principle that every man belonged to some woman. A bachelor ought to be devoted to his mother or sister. A widower should keep on belonging to the wife he had lost.

This last belief was one that she often tried to implant in Father. He had every intention of outliving her, if he could, and she knew it. He said it was only his devotion to her that made him feel this way—he didn't see how she could get on without him, and he must stay alive to take care of her. Mother snorted at this benevolent attitude. She said she could get on perfectly well, but of course she'd die long before he did. And what worried her was how he'd behave himself when she was gone.

One day in an ancient chapel near Oxford, they were shown a tomb where a noble crusader was buried, with his effigy laid out on top. Mother was much impressed till the verger pointed to the figure beside him, of the lady who had been his third wife. Mother immediately struck at the tomb with her parasol, demanding, "Where's your first, you old thing!"

The verger was so shocked that he wouldn't show them the rest of the church; but Mother didn't want to see it anyway. She told the verger he ought to be ashamed of himself for exhibiting an old wretch like that, and she went out at once, feeling strongly that it was no place for Father.

CHAPTER 24

FATHER AMONG THE POTTED PALMS

ALTHOUGH FATHER enjoyed himself when Mother and he went to parties, the idea of giving a party in his own home seemed monstrous. The most he would consent to was to have a few old friends in to dinner. He said that when Mother went beyond that, she turned the whole place upside down. He said he declined to have his comfort "set at naught" in that manner.

Father put comfort first in his home life: he had plenty of adventure downtown. But Mother got tired of dining with nobody but his old friends all the time. She wanted to see different houses, new people. By temperament she was an explorer.

She knew that an explorer who got no invitations to explore sat at home. And the surest way to get invitations was to give them, and to all sorts of people, and turn Father's home upside down whether he liked it or not.

To forestall opposition, Mother's method was to invite one couple whom Father knew, so that when he looked around the table one or two of the faces would be familiar, but as to the others she experimented. If questioned by Father as to who'd be there, she said, "Why, the Bakers, and I hope a few others." This reassured him till the night of the dinner arrived. Then, when he came home and found potted palms in the hall, it was too late to stop her.

That dinner for "the Bakers and a few others" was a dinner of ten, and the principal guests were the Ormontons, whom Mother had been determined to invite ever since she had met them. She didn't really know what they were like yet, but they had looked most imposing.

One night just a week before the event, we heard a ring at the front door. It was about seven o'clock. We were just finishing our six-o'clock dinner. Mother had come in so late from the Horse Show that she hadn't bothered to dress; she had thrown off her frock on her bed and slipped into a wrapper. Bridget, the waitress, an awkward girl whose mouth dropped wide open in crises, went to answer the bell.

We heard her open the door. Then, in the silence, there was the sound of somebody going upstairs. We looked in surprise at one another. Only dinner guests ever went up automatically that way, expecting to take off their coats and wraps in some upper bedroom.

Mother leapt from her chair and ran out to the hall. She had guessed what was happening. Sure enough, there was Bridget, staring helplessly with her mouth gaping open, at two stately figures, the Ormontons, resplendently marching upstairs.

At the head of those stairs was Mother's bedroom, in the wildest disorder. Another moment and Mrs. Ormonton would have gone in there to take off her wraps. "Why, Mrs. Ormonton!" Mother called, in a panic. "Haven't you made a mistake?"

The march upward was halted. The two dignified figures looked solemnly over the banisters.

"It's *next* Tuesday that you're coming to dine!" Mother cried, clutching in dismay at her wrapper.

Mr. Ormonton stared disapprovingly at Mother a moment. Then, as he began to take in what had happened, he pursed his lips, his eyes popped, and he turned and scowled at his wife. She looked at him in fright and slumped slowly, like a soft tallow candle.

"*Next* Tuesday," Mother faintly repeated.

The Ormontons pulled themselves together and came slowly down.

They stood helplessly in the hall by the hatrack. As they had dismissed their carriage, they had no way to remove themselves from our home. A streetcar was impossible for an Ormonton in full evening dress. They would have to wait till a cab could be sent for, which would take at least half an hour and probably more.

If we could have offered them some impromptu little meal, it might have been welcome to both of them, but we boys had eaten every last scrap, and Mother couldn't think how to manage it. She didn't feel she knew them well enough to have that awful Bridget bring up some cold meat and a glass of milk and an old piece of pie. So they waited in their sumptuous clothes, cross and wretched and hungry. They had little or no sense of fun, even in their happiest moments, and they certainly did not feel light-hearted as they sat in out parlor. Mother had to make conversation, in her wrapper, till almost eight o'clock. Mr. Ormonton said nothing whatever. He felt too much wronged, too indignant. Father strolled in and offered him a cigar. It was stiffly declined.

A week later, when they again rang the bell, they were stiffer than ever. But by that time our easy-going household was completely transformed. Instead of Bridget and her elbows, a butler suavely opened the door. Large potted palms stood in the hall. The Ormontons felt more at home.

They could not have imagined how much work Mother's preparations had cost. To begin with, she had gone to a little shop she had found on Sixth Avenue, under the Elevated, a place where they sold delicious ice cream and French pastries and bonbons, which was run by a pleasant and enterprising young man named Louis Sherry. He had arranged to send over old John, a waiter, to be our butler *pro tem,* and a greasy and excitable young chef to take charge of our kitchen, and they had brought with them neat covered baskets which they wouldn't let us boys touch.

Old John and Mother had a great deal to do in the dining-room: getting out arsenals of silver to be laid at each place, putting leaves in the black-walnut table, filling vases with flowers, arranging little plates of salted almonds and chocolates, and I don't know what else. The heavy plush furniture in the parlor had to be rearranged, too, and piles of special plates taken down from the pantry top shelf, and an elaborately embroidered tablecloth and napkins got out of the linen closet. And after Mother had run around all day attending to these, and had laid out the right dress and slippers, and done things to her hair, she had ended by desperately tackling the worst job of all, which was to put her bedroom in order.

This room, in spite of Mother's random efforts, had an obstinate habit of never being as neat and pretty-looking as she wished it to be. On the contrary, it was always getting into a comfortable, higgledy-piggledy state. And every time Mother gave a dinner, she felt guiltily sure that the ladies who took off their wraps in it would have gimlet eyes. Everything, therefore, had to be put away out of sight. Her plan was to do this so neatly that any drawer which these prying creatures might open would be in beautiful order. But she never had time enough, so after the first two or three drawers had had their upper levels fixed up, things were pushed into the others any which way, and when she was through they were locked. Letters and pieces of string were hurried off the dressing-table, medicines and change off the mantel, stray bits of lace, pencils, veils, and old macaroons off the bureau. Some were jammed into cabinets that were already so full they could hardly be shut, some disappeared into hatboxes or were poked up on dark closet shelves. Among these jumbled articles were many that would be urgently needed next week, but by that time even Mother couldn't remember where on earth she had put them, and she spent hours hunting hopelessly for a lost glove or key. When the bedroom was "picked up" at last, it had lost its old friendly air. A splendid spread lay on the bed smoothly. The bolster and pillows were covered as elaborately as if no one used them to sleep on. A big china kerosene lamp and some pink-shaded candles were lit. And Mother, all tired out, was being laced up the back in her tight-fitting gown.

Father had none of this work to do in his room. In fact he had no work at all. He dressed for dinner every night anyhow, and his room was always in order. Everything he owned had its place, and he never laid his clothes down at random. There were two drawers for his shirts, for example, another drawer for his socks, his shaving-kit was always on his English shaving-stand by the window. On his bureau were a pair of military hairbrushes, two combs, and a bottle of bay rum—nothing else. Each of his books had its own allotted place on his shelves. And on each shelf and in every drawer there was extra room. Nothing was crowded.

When he undressed to go to bed, he began by taking the things out of his pockets and putting them into a little drawer which he reserved for that purpose. He then hung his suit on its own regular hook in his closet and laid his underwear in the washbasket. He never left anything lying around on the chairs. He did these things so swiftly that he could dress or undress in ten minutes, and when he turned out the gas and opened his big window, his room was as trim as a general's.

On the night of the dinner, he came home at his usual hour, swore at the potted palms, and took John down to the cellar to get out the right wines. Then he went to his room; and as dinner was later than usual, he had a short nap. He got up a quarter of an hour or so before it was time for the guests to arrive, screwed in his studs, shaved and dressed, gave his white tie a sharp, exact twist, and peacefully went down to the parlor. Finding Mother there, adjusting a smoky lamp, he said he'd be damned if he'd stand it, having his comfort interfered with by a lot of people he did not wish to see. He added that if they didn't come on time, they needn't expect him to wait—he was hungry.

But the guests soon began clattering up to our door over the cobblestones in their broughams, and Father smiled at the men and shook hands warmly with the best-looking women, and got all their names mixed up, imperturbably, until John opened the great sliding doors of the little dining-room, and they went in to dinner.

As for the rest of the evening, it was just another dinner for Father, except that he had sherry and champagne instead of claret, and some dishes by a good chef. But Mother, looking critically around at her social material, and watching the service every minute, had to work to the last. No matter how formal and wooden her material was, it was her business to stir them to life and make the atmosphere jolly. She usually succeeded, she was so darting and gay, but on this high occasion some of the guests couldn't be made to unbend.

Father didn't notice that they were wooden, nor did he feel disappointed. With a good dinner and sound wines inside him, he could enjoy any climate. He also enjoyed talking to people about whatever came into his head, and he seldom bothered to observe if they listened or how they responded.

Bridget's duties were to stay in the pantry and help John and keep quiet. She stayed in the pantry all right, but she flunked on the rest of it. Each time that she dropped something, she made a loud, gasping sound. John went on about his business, ignoring this in a severe and magnificent manner, but nobody else was quite able to, except, of course, Father. To Mother's relief, he unconsciously saved the day for her by being too absorbed in his own conversation to hear these weird interruptions.

The climax came at dessert. By that time, Bridget was completely demoralized, and she so far forgot herself as to poke her face outside the screen and hiss some question hoarsely at John. An awful silence came over the table. But Father, who felt as astonished as anybody, took no pains to conceal it. He turned squarely around and demanded: "What the devil's that noise?"

Father's utter naturalness made even Mr. Ormonton smile. All formality melted away, to Mother's surprise and delight, and though Father had no idea he had caused it, a gay evening began.

CHAPTER 25

FATHER HAS A BAD NIGHT

ONE WINTER morning when Father left the Riding Club on horseback and rode through East Fifty-eighth Street, his horse fell with him. Not only did the stupid animal fall but he landed on Father's foot.

Father pulled his foot out from under, got the horse up, and went on to the Park for his ride. But he found later that one of his toes had been bent and that he couldn't straighten it out.

This was not only an inconvenience to Father, it was a surprise. He knew other men got smashed up in accidents, but he had assumed that that was because they were brittle. He wasn't. He was constructed in such a manner, he had supposed, that he couldn't be damaged. He still believed that this was the case. Yet one of his toes had got bent.

That toe never did straighten out and Father talked of it often. He felt that he had had a strange experience, one that was against Nature's laws, and he expected those who listened to his story to be deeply concerned and impressed. If they weren't, he repeated it.

We heard it at home hundreds of times, one year after another. "That's enough about your toe," Mother would cry. "Nobody cares about your toe, you know, Clare!"

But Father said that of course people did. He told all his friends at the club. "You know what happened to me? Why, one morning when the pavement was icy, that bay cob that Sam Babcock sold me fell on my toe—and he *bent* it! Never had such a thing happen to me all my life. Bent my toe! It's getting a corn on it now. Here. On top. My shoemaker says he can't fix it. There's nobody as stupid as a shoemaker, except that bay cob."

From this time on, although he still was contemptuous of diseases, Father began to dislike to hear any accounts of other men's accidents. They seemed to him portents of what might happen, even to him.

One day in the country, when he took the train at the Harrison station, he saw a pretty neighbor of ours, young Mrs. Wainwright, sitting in the car with her boy. He stopped to say how d'ye do, intending to sit and talk with her. But she said, as she greeted him, "I'm taking my little son in to the dentist—he's had such a sad accident, Mr. Day. He's broken off two front teeth."

The boy grinned, Father looked at the broken stumps, and his face got all twisted and shocked. "Oh, my God!" he said. "Oh! Oh!" And he hurriedly left her, to sit in some other car. When he got home that evening, he complained about this occurrence, and blamed Mrs. Wainwright for showing him her family horrors.

"Your husband felt so badly about my little boy," Mrs. Wainwright said next week to Mother. "How sympathetic he is, Mrs. Day."

A year or so later, Father had another of these situations to face. The doctors had to operate on one of my legs for adhesions. Worst of all, since for some reason I couldn't be moved at that time to a hospital, I was operated on at home.

They left me feeling comfortable enough, with my leg trussed up in plaster. But Mother was troubled and unhappy about it, and when Father came in and she ran to him to pour out her woes she disturbed him.

He couldn't get away from it this time. There was no next car to go to. He puckered his face up in misery. He chucked his coat and hat in the closet. He finally told Mother he was sorry for me but he wished she would let him be sorry in peace. The whole damn house was upset, he said, and he wanted his dinner.

When he had his dinner, he couldn't enjoy it. He could only half enjoy his cigar. He felt distressed but didn't wish to say so. He was cross to Mother. He swore. Mother said he was heartless and went off to bed.

He felt badly to think that I might be suffering. But he didn't at all like to feel badly. He didn't know much about suffering, and the whole situation confused him. He walked up and down and said "Damn." He said he wished to God that people would take care of themselves the way he did, and be healthy and not bother him this way. Then he lit another cigar, sat down to read, and tried to forget all about it. But as his feelings wouldn't let him do that, he helplessly frowned at his book.

Mother had told him not to go up to see me, but after a while he just had to. He came quietly up to the top floor, groped around in the dark, and looked in my door. "Well, my dear boy," he said.

His voice was troubled and tender.

I said, "Hello, Father."

That made him feel a little better, and he hopefully asked me, "How are you?"

I made an effort and replied, "I'm all right."

"Oh, damn," Father said, and went down again.

I knew it was the wrong thing to say. If I had been angry at my leg and the ether, he would have felt reassured. He liked a man to be brave in a good, honest, full-blooded way. He hated to see him merely lie still and pretend he was all right when he wasn't.

He sat up late, smoking and reading or pacing the floor, and when he went to bed himself he slept badly. That was the last straw.

He got up and moved into the spare room in the rear of the house. I was in the room just above. I could hear him talking bitterly to himself about the way they had tucked in the sheets. Even after he had got them fixed properly, his mind was not at rest. He tossed impatiently about, got up and drank some water, said it was too warm, dozed a little, woke up again, hunted around for the switch, turned the light on, and felt miserable. As he never did anything in silence, his resentment burst out in groans. They grew louder and louder.

My leg was feeling easier by that time. I had no pain to speak of, and I slept all that Father would let me. Mother, on the floor below Father, with her ears stuffed with cotton, slept too. But the spare-room bed was by an open window facing the quiet back yards, and as the neighbors, it seemed, had no cotton, they hadn't much chance to rest.

The next day, Mother happened to stop in to see Mrs. Crane, who lived a few doors away from us, and started to tell her about my operation. But Mrs. Crane interrupted.

"Oh yes, Mrs. Day," she said. "My daughter and I knew something had happened. It must have been terrible. We were so sorry for him. We could hear him groaning all night. How very hard it must have been for you. My daughter and I got a little sleep toward morning, but I'm afraid you had none at all."

On her way home, Mother met another of the neighbors, Mrs. Robbins, who lived on the other side of our block in the next street, and whose rear bedrooms faced ours. Mrs. Robbins, too, knew all about it.

"My room is in the front of the house," she said, "so I didn't know what had happened until Mr. Robbins told me at breakfast. He talked of nothing else all this morning. He couldn't believe that I hadn't heard the—er—your poor son's dreadful cries."

Mother waited that evening for Father to get home from his office. The minute he came in, she pounced on him. "Oh, *Clare!*" she said. "I am so ashamed of you! You get worse and worse. I saw

Mrs. Crane today and Mrs. Robbins, and they told me what happened last night, and I don't believe any of the neighbors got one wink of sleep."

"Well," Father answered, "neither did I."

"Yes, but Clare," Mother impatiently cried, seizing his coat lapels and trying to shake him, "they thought it was Clarence making those noises and all the time it was you!"

"I don't give a damn what they thought," Father said wearily. "I had a bad night."

CHAPTER 26

FATHER AND HIS OTHER SELVES

FATHER'S ATTITUDE toward anybody who wasn't his kind used to puzzle me. It was so dictatorial. There was no live and let live about it. And to make it worse he had no compunctions about any wounds he inflicted; on the contrary, he felt that people should be grateful to him for teaching them better.

This was only one side of him, of course, as I realized better later, for I saw even more of him after I grew up than I had in my childhood. He was one of the jolliest and most companionable men I ever knew. He always seemed to have a good time when he went to the club. He liked most of the men whom he met there, and they felt that same way toward him. One or another of them walked home with him, usually, and stood talking with him by the front stoop. And when he rode with his friends in the Park or went for a sail on some yacht, or when he and his fellow-directors of some little railroad spent a week on a tour of inspection, they came back full of fun.

It was only with men of his own sort that he did this, however. They understood him and he them. They all had an air and a feeling, in those days, of enormous authority. When they disagreed, it was often quite violently, but that didn't matter. At bottom they thoroughly approved of and respected each other.

Toward people with whom he didn't get on well, though, he was imperious, and when they displeased or annoyed him, it made him snort like a bull.

I disapproved of this strongly when I was a boy. It seemed natural to me that any father should snort, more or less, about the behavior of his wife, or his children, or his relatives generally. It seemed natural, too, for a man to make his employees live exactly as he decreed. That sort of thing was so much in the air that I, for one, didn't question it. But Father didn't stop there; he expected everyone else to conform, even people he read about in the newspapers. Even historical characters. He never failed to denounce them indignantly when he found that they hadn't.

He felt the same way about persons he passed in the street. And sometimes in a horse-car he looked around at his fellow-passengers like a colonel distastefully reviewing a slatternly regiment. They didn't all have to be bankers or lawyers or clubmen—though if they were, all the better—but they did have to be neat and decent. And self-respecting. Like him. He would glare at men whose vests were unbuttoned, or whose neckties were loose, or whose general appearance was sloppy, as though they deserved hanging. He said he hated slovenly people. He said that they were "offensive."

"What difference does it make to you, Father?" I'd ask him. He didn't explain. I could have understood his quietly disliking them, for a sense of the fitness of things was strong in him; but why did he feel so much heat?

One day I came upon a magazine article which discussed this very matter. No ego ought to feel entirely separate, the writer explained. It should think of others as its own alter egos—differing forms of itself. This wasn't at all the way I looked at others. I expected nearly all of them to be different and I was surprised when they weren't. This magazine writer said that only unsocial persons felt that way. Well, at least this idea made Father's attitude understandable to me. If he was simply thinking of others as his own other selves, that might be why, when they didn't behave as such, he got in a passion about it.

Every morning Father sat in the big armchair in the dining-room window to look over his newspaper and see just what his alter egos had been up to since yesterday. If they hadn't been up to anything, he turned to the financial page or read one or two editorials—one or two being all he could stand, because he said they were wishy-washy. If, however, the Mayor had been faithless again to Father's ideals, or if Tammany Hall had done anything at all, good or bad, Father ringingly denounced these atrocities to us little boys and to Mother.

For a long time none of the rest of us joined in these political talks. This suited Father exactly. He didn't wish to be hindered, or even helped, when he was letting off steam. After a while, though, Mother began attending a class in current events, which an enterprising young woman, a Miss Edna Gulick, conducted on Tuesdays. Social, musical, and literary matters took up most of Miss Gulick's mind. But though she didn't go deeply into politics or industrial problems, merely darting about on the surface in a bright, sprightly way, she did this so skillfully, and made everything seem so clear to Mother, that the most baffling and intricate issues became childishly simple.

The day after one of these classes, just when Father was wholeheartedly bombarding President Benjamin Harrison and somebody named William McKinley for putting through a new tariff and trying their best to ruin the country, Mother boldly chimed in. She said she was sure that the President's idea was all right; he had only been a little unfortunate in the way he had put it.

Father laid down his paper in high displeasure. "What do *you* know about it?" he demanded.

"Miss Gulick says she has it on the best authority," Mother firmly declared. "She says the President prays to God for guidance, and that he is a very good-hearted man."

"The President," said Father, "is a nincompoop, and I strongly suspect he's a scalawag, and I wish to God you wouldn't talk on matters you don't know a damned thing about."

"I do too know about them," Mother exclaimed. "Miss Gulick says every intelligent woman should have some opinion—about this tariff thing, and capital and labor, and everything else."

"Well I'll be damned," Father said in amazement. "Who, may I ask, is Miss Gulick?"

"Why, she's that current-events person I told you about, and the tickets are a dollar each Tuesday," said Mother.

"Do you mean to tell me that a pack of idle-minded females pay a dollar apiece to hear another female gabble about the events of the day?" Father asked. "Listen to *me* if you want to know anything about the events of the day."

"But you get so excited, Clare dear, and you always talk so long and so loud that I never can see what you're getting at. About tariffs. And strikes."

"It is a citizen's duty," Father began, getting angrily into his overcoat, but Mother wouldn't be interrupted.

"Another reason that we all like Miss Gulick so much," she went on, "is that she says kindness is much more important than arguments. And she says that it makes her feel very sad when she reads about strikes, because capital and labor could easily learn to be nice to each other."

Father burst out of the house, banging the door, and finished buttoning his coat on the top step of our stoop. "I don't know what the world is coming to anyhow," I heard him exclaim to a few surprised passers-by on quiet Madison Avenue.

CHAPTER 27

FATHER FINDS GUESTS
IN THE HOUSE

FATHER WAS a sociable man; he liked to sit and talk with us at home, or with his friends at the club. And in summer he permitted guests to stay with us out in the country, where there was plenty of room for them, and where he sometimes used to feel lonely. But in town he regarded any prolonged hospitality as a sign of weak natures. He felt that in town he must be stern with would-be houseguests or he'd be overrun with them. He had no objection to callers who dropped in for a cup of tea and got out, but when a guest came to our door with a handbag—or, still worse, a trunk——he said it was a damned imposition.

What complicated the matter was that nobody stayed with us usually except Mother's relatives. Father's relatives were well-regulated New Yorkers who stayed in their own homes, and he often told Mother that the sooner hers learned to, the better.

He had strong feelings about this and they always seemed to come out with a bang. When he got home for dinner and when Mother was obliged to confess that some of her relatives were concealed in

the spare room, up on the third floor, those relatives were likely to
wonder what was the matter downstairs. If Mother hadn't slammed
the door, they would have heard indignant roars about locusts that
ought to be sent back to Egypt instead of settling on Father.

Most of the guests had good consciences, however, and had been
led to suppose Father loved them; and as they themselves were hospitable persons who would have welcomed him at their homes,
they didn't suspect that those muffled outcries were occasioned by
them. They merely felt sorry that poor Father was feeling upset
about something. Mother encouraged them in this attitude; she said
Father was worried about things and they must pretend not to notice.
When Father glared speechlessly around the table at dinner, they
felt sorrier for him than ever. Aunt Emma, who was a placid soul,
once asked him if he had ever tried Dicer's Headache Lozenges,
which were excellent in moments of depression and had also helped
her anemia. Father nearly burst a blood vessel telling her that he
was not anemic.

One of the things that Father especially detested about guests
was the suddenness with which they arrived. So far as he knew, they
invariably came without warning. The reason Mother never told
him in advance was that he'd then have had two explosions—one
when he was forbidding their coming, and one when they came.

Father made repeated attempts to acquaint Mother with his
views about guests. This objectionable tribe, he explained to her,
had two bad characteristics. One was that they didn't seem to know
enough to go to hotels. New York was full of such structures, he
pointed out, designed for the one special purpose of housing these
nuisances. If they got tired of hotels, he said, they should be put
aboard the next train at once, and shipped to some large, empty
desert. If they wanted to roam, the damn gipsies, lend 'em a hand,
keep 'em roaming.

But a still more annoying habit they had, he said, was that they
wanted to be entertained, and every single one of them seemed to
expect him to do it. Not content with disrupting the orderly routine

of his household and ringing the bell every minute and sitting too long in his bathtub, they tried to make him go gallivanting off with them to a restaurant or give up his after-dinner cigar to see some long-winded play. He said to Mother, "I wish you to understand clearly that I am not a Swiss courier. I must decline to conduct groups of strangers around town at night. You can tell Emma that it is my desire to live here in peace, and that I do not intend to hold a perpetual Mardi Gras to please gaping villagers."

We didn't have visitors often, but still we did have a spare room. In this chamber was a little round fireplace, with a grate sticking out of it, surmounted by a white marble mantel. The mantel would have looked cold and tomblike if left to itself, but hanging from its edge there was a strip of red velvet about six inches deep, with a wavy gold border. On the mantel was a pink porcelain clock, trimmed with gilt, with a sweet-toned French bell. Two graceful though urn-like pink vases stood at the ends of the mantel, and on each side of the clock was a large Dresden figure. One was a curtseying shep-herdess with a small waist, in a pink-and-green petticoat, and opposite her there danced a rosy shepherd, with one arm gone, playing away on a pipe.

The walls and carpet were dark. At each window were two sets of curtains, one lacy and white and one of thick silk brocade. The tiebacks consisted of elaborate loops with big tassels.

The principal pieces of furniture were a solid black mahogany bureau, tall and heavily carved, and a bed to match, so broad that it could have easily held several guests. Beside the bed stood a square black commode, with a white marble top.

This room, although somber, seemed waiting to be lived in; it had an air of dignified welcome. But when a guest started to inves-tigate, he found that this was misleading. Except for the top of the bureau, there was really no place to put things. Every drawer was filled to bursting already with the overflow of other rooms. One of the two big closets was locked. In the other were ball dresses, an umbrella stand, piles of magazines, a small pair of steps, a job lot of discarded bonnets, and a painting of old Mr. Howe. After taking a good look at this closet, a guest generally gave up all hope of unpacking and resigned himself politely to camping out the best way he could.

His mind had little opportunity, however, to dwell on these small inconveniences, for he soon became engrossed by the drama of our family life. Our disconcerting inability to conceal any of our emotions absorbed him.

I never supposed that our daily lives were different from anyone else's until I went off on visits myself. At Jeff Barry's home, when I saw his dignified old parents being formally polite to each other, I thought they were holding themselves tightly in, and I used to wonder which of them would blow up first. I was relieved yet depressed when they didn't. They were so gentle and had such quiet ways that they seemed to me lifeless.

On a visit to the McGillians, I was shocked to discover that a married pair could be mean to each other. Even their children made sarcastic and biting remarks, as though they were trying to hurt one another in what I thought an underhand way. All our family got hurt often enough, but at least it wasn't deliberate. Our collisions were impulsive and open. We all had red hair and got angry in a second, but in a minute or two it was over.

Another family whose customs seemed strange to me was Johnny Clark's. Professor Clark, Johnny's father, when he was annoyed wouldn't speak. Around the first of the month, when the bills came in, he would sit without saying a word all through dinner, looking down at his plate. After we boys left the room, we heard Mrs. Clark beg him to tell her what she was to do. She said she was willing to live in a tent and spend nothing if he would only be pleasant. Mr. Clark listened to her in silence and then went off to his study.

This seemed to me gruesome. In our household, things got pretty rough at times but at least we had no black gloom. Our home life was stormy but spirited. It always had tang. When Father was unhappy, he said so. He poured out his grief with such vigor that it soon cleared the air.

If he had ever had any meannesses in him, he might have tried to repress them. But he was a thoroughly good-hearted and warm-blooded man, and he saw no reason for hiding his feelings. They were too strong to hide anyway.

One day while Father was in his office downtown, Auntie Gussie and Cousin Flossie arrived. Mother immediately began planning to take them to dine at the Waldorf, a much-talked-of new hotel at Fifth Avenue and Thirty-third Street, which she very much wanted to see. She knew Father mightn't like the idea, but he would enjoy himself after he got there, and she thought she could manage him.

When he came in, she went to his bedroom to break the good news to him that instead of dining at home he was to go off on a gay little party. She meant to do this diplomatically. But she wasn't an adept at coaxing or inveigling a man, and even if she had been, Father was not at all easy to coax. Whenever she was planning to manage him, the very tone of her voice put him on guard; it had an impatient note, as though really the only plan she could think of was to wish he was manageable. So on this occasion, when she tried to get him in a good mood, he promptly got in a bad one. He looked suspiciously at Mother and said, "I don't feel well."

"You need a little change," Mother said. "That'll make you feel better. Besides, Gussie's here and she wants to dine with us tonight at the Waldorf."

Father hated surprise attacks of this kind. No matter how placid he might be, he instantly got hot when one came. In less than a second he was rending the Waldorf asunder and saying what he thought of anybody who wanted to dine there.

But Mother was fully prepared to see him take it hard at the start. She paid no attention to his vehement refusals. She said brightly that the Waldorf was lovely and that it would do him good to go out. There was no dinner at home for him anyway, so what else was there to do?

When Father took in the situation, he undressed and put on his nightshirt. He shouted angrily at Mother that he had a sick headache.

It made no difference to him whether there was any dinner or not. He couldn't touch a mouthful of food, he declared. Food be damned. What he needed was rest. After tottering around, putting his clothes away, he darkened his room. He climbed into bed. He pulled up the sheets, and he let out his breath in deep groans.

These startling blasts, which came at regular intervals, alarmed Auntie Gussie. But when she hurried down to help, Mother seemed annoyed and shooed her back up.

The next thing she knew, Mother impatiently called up to her that she was waiting. She had got tired of scolding Father and trying to make him get out of bed, and had made up her mind to dine at the Waldorf without him. She and Auntie Gussie and Flossie marched off by themselves. But they had to come back almost immediately because Mother didn't have enough money, and when she rushed into Father's sick-room and lit the gas again and made him get up and give her ten dollars, his roars of pain were terrific.

After they went out, his groans lessened in volume and were presently succeeded by snores. Father had a good nap. When he woke up, he felt happier. He said his headache was gone. He came downstairs in his dressing-gown and slippers, and sent for some bread and milk. He ate several huge bowlfuls of it with gusto, peacefully smoked a cigar, and was back in his bed again, reading, when Mother came home.

CHAPTER 28

FATHER AND HIS PET RUG

FATHER LIKED spending his summers in the country, once he had got used to it, but it introduced two major earthquakes each year into his life. One when he moved out of town in the spring, and one in the fall when he moved back. If there was one thing Father hated it was packing. It seemed a huddled, irregular affair to a man with his orderly mind. For a week or more before it was time to begin he was upset by the prospect. He had only a few drawers full of clothes to empty into a trunk, but it had to be done in a certain particular way. No one else could attend to it for him— no one else could do the thing properly. All that Mother could do was to have his trunk brought to his room. When it had been laid in a corner, gaping at him, his groaning began. He walked around, first putting his shirts in, then his clothes and his underwear, then burrowing under and taking some out again to go in the suitcase, then deciding that after all he would not take part of what he had packed. During all such perplexities he communed with himself, not in silence.

The first sounds that used to come from his room were low
groans of self-pity. Later on, as the task he was struggling with became
more and more complicated, he could be heard stamping about,
and denouncing his garments. If we looked in his door we would
see him in the middle of the room with a bathrobe, which had
already been packed twice in the suitcase and once in the trunk,
and which was now being put back in the trunk again because the
suitcase was crowded. Later it would once more go back in the suitcase so as to be where he could get at it. His face was red and angry,
and he was earnestly saying, "Damnation!"

Long before any of this began Mother had already started her
end of it. Father packed only his own clothes. She packed everything else: except that she had someone to help her, of course, with
the heavy things. In the fall, for instance, a man named Jerome
sometimes went up to the country to do this. He was a taciturn,
preoccupied colored man, an expert at moving, who worked so well
and quickly that he kept getting ahead of his schedule. It was distracting to Mother to plan out enough things to keep Jerome busy.
It was also distracting to see him sit idle. He was paid by the day.

But the principal problem that Mother had to attend to was Father.
He said that he didn't really mind moving but that he did object to
the fuss. As to rugs, for instance, he refused to have any at all put away
until after he and all his belongings had been moved from the house.
This seemed unreasonable to me—I said he ought to allow them to
make a beginning and put a few away, surely. He would admit, pri-
vately, that this was true perhaps, but here was the trouble: if he once
let Mother get started she would go much too far. "When your mother
is closing up a house," he said, "she gets too absorbed in it. She is apt
to forget my comfort entirely—and also her own. I have found by
experience that if I yield an inch in this matter the place is all torn
up." He added that he had to insist upon absolute order, simply
because the alternative was absolute chaos. Furthermore, why
shouldn't the process be orderly if it were skillfully handled? If it wasn't,
it was no fault of his, and he declined to be made to suffer for it.

Mother's side of it was that it was impossible to move out imperceptibly. "Things naturally get upset a little, Clare dear, when you're making a change. If they get upset too much I can't help it; and I do wish you would stop bothering me."

One result of this difference was a war about the rugs every fall. Two or three weeks before they left, Mother always had the large rug in the hall taken up—there was no need of *two* rugs in the hall, she told Father.

"I won't have it, damn it, you're making the place a barracks," he said.

"But we're *moving,*" Mother expostulated; "we must get the house closed."

"Close it properly then! Do things suitably, without this cursed helter-skelter." He retreated into the library where he could sit by a fire, while Mother went in and out of cold rooms and halls with her shawl on.

The library had two large heavy pieces of furniture in it—a grand piano, and a huge desklike table piled with papers and books. This table filled the center of the room and stood square on a rug. It was hard work to lift that heavy table to get the rug out from under it. Until this was done, every year, Mother kept thinking about it at night. Strictly speaking, it wasn't necessary to have that rug put away much beforehand, but she wanted to get it over and done with so that she could sleep. But Father was particularly dependent on this rug because he liked to sit in the library; he was always determined that it shouldn't be touched till he left.

He couldn't, however, remain on guard continuously. He sometimes had to go out. In fact he was maneuvered into going out, though this he never quite learned. In the late afternoon when he supposed the day's activities over, he would come out of the library and venture to go off in the motor. Not far, just to get the evening paper, which was a very short trip. His mind was quiet: he assumed that nothing much could be done in his absence. But just as he was leaving he would be given some errand to do—some provisions to buy in the next town beyond, or a book to leave at some friend's. Or if this might make him suspicious, nothing would be said as he left, but the chauffeur would be given instructions what to say when he had bought Father's paper.

"There are some flowers in the car, sir, that Mrs. Day . . . "

Father looked up from his paper, and looked threateningly over his glasses. "What's all this?" he said. *"What?"*

The chauffeur repeated mildly "—that Mrs. Day wishes left at the church."

"Damn the church," Father answered, going back to the market reports. Not that he was down on that institution, he believed in it firmly, but he expected the church to behave itself and not interfere with his drives. However, he was looking through his paper, and he didn't say no, and the chauffeur didn't give him time to anyhow, but cranked up the car, and off they went down the Post Road, all the way into Rye.

When they got home, Father hung up his overcoat in the cold hall, and grasping his evening paper he marched back to the library fire. . . .

Meantime things had been happening. Mother had had the big table lifted, and had got up the rug; and Jerome had lugged it out to the laundry yard to beat it. After that, his orders were to roll it and wrap it and put it away. While he was doing this, which was naturally expected to take him some time, Mother thankfully went up to the china room to pack certain cups. She always felt a little more peaceful when Jerome was fully occupied. . . .

A little later, when she was in her own room and had just sat down for a minute, for the first time that day, and was sorting the linen, and humming, there was a knock at the door.

Mother sat up sharply, every bit of her alert again. "Who is that?"

She heard a deprecating little cough, then Jerome's quiet voice. "Now—er—Mrs. Day?"

"Well, what *is* it, Jerome?" Mother wailed. She had thought she had left that man enough to do for once anyhow, but here he was

back on her hands again. "What is it *now?*" she said in despair. "Have
you finished that work?"

"No'm," Jerome said reassuringly. "I ain't finished that yet." He
paused, and coughed again, conscious that he was bringing poor
news. "Mr. Day, he's hollerin' consid'able, down in the liberry."

"What about? What's the matter with him?"

Jerome knew she knew well enough. He said "Yes'm," mechan-
ically; and added in a worried way, as if to himself, "He's a-hollerin'
for that rug."

Mother didn't like Jerome to use that word, "hollerin'." It
wasn't respectful. But it was so painfully descriptive that she couldn't
think what other word he could substitute. She put down the linen.
I never could see why she didn't stay quietly in her room, at such
moments, and let Father keep up his hollerin' till he cooled off. But
I was an outsider in these wars, and Mother of course was a com-
batant. She charged out into the big upper hall, and at once began
an attack, launching her counter-offensive vigorously, over the banisters. She called loudly upon Father to stop right away and be still;
and she told him how wicked it was of him to make trouble for her
when she was working so hard. Father, from his post in the library,
boomed a violent reply. It was like an artillery bombardment. Neither side could see the other. But they fired great guns with great
vigor, and it all seemed in earnest.

Jerome stood respectfully waiting, wondering how it would come
out. He was wholly in the dark as to which side was winning, there
was so much give and take. But the combatants knew. Mother
presently saw she was beaten. There was some note she detected in
Father's voice, deeper than bluster; or some weariness in herself that
betrayed her. At any rate, she gave in.

She turned to Jerome. He saw that she was thinking how she
could fix it. Jerome felt dejected. Had that big old rug got to be
toted back into the library?

"Jerome, I'll have to give Mr. Day one of those rugs from the blue
room—one of the long narrow white fur pair. You know which I mean?"

"Yes'm," Jerome said with partial relief. "Put it under that desk?"

"No, between the desk and the fireplace. By Mr. Day's chair. That's all that's necessary. He just wants something under his feet."

This wasn't at all Father's idea of what he wanted, as Jerome soon discovered, when he took the long white fur rug down to him. Father was so completely amazed he forgot to be angry. He had supposed he had won that bombardment. He had made Mother cease firing. Yet now after he had lowered his temperature again back to normal, and settled down to enjoy the fruits of his victory, namely his own big square rug, here was Jerome bringing him instead a long narrow hairy monstrosity.

"What's that?" he demanded.

Jerome limply exhibited the monstrosity, feeling hopeless inside, like a pessimistic salesman with no confidence in his own goods.

"What are you bringing that thing in here for?"

"Yessir, Mr. Day. Mrs. Day says put it under your feet."

Father started to turn loose his batteries all over again. But his guns had gone cold. He felt plenty of disgust and exasperation, but not quite enough fury. He fired what he had at Jerome, who stood up to it silently; and he kicked the offending white fur rug, and said he wouldn't have it. But something in the air now seemed to tell him, in his turn, he had lost. Even Jerome felt this, and put the rug under his feet, "temporary," leaving Father trying to read his paper again, indignant and bitter. He particularly disliked this white rug. He remembered it now from last year.

Mother went back to the linen. The house became quiet. The only sounds were thuds in the laundry yard, where Jerome was at work, beating and sweeping his booty, concealed by the hedge.

By the library fire Father was turning over the page of his paper, and glaring at the white rug, and saying to himself loudly, "I hate it!" He kicked at the intruder. "Damn woolly thing. I want my own rug."

CHAPTER 29

FATHER AND THE
FRENCH COURT

EXCEPT IN his very last years, when he began to get shaky, Father wasn't bored in his old age, like some men. He kept up his billiards, enjoying the hard shots, until his eye grew less true; and he always found it absorbing to try to beat himself at solitaire. He enjoyed his drives until automobiles came and ruined the roads with their crowding. He enjoyed having a go at the morning paper, in a thoroughly combative spirit. Every time the President said or did anything which got on the front page, Father either commended him—in surprise—for having some backbone for once, or else said he was an infernal scoundrel and ought to be kicked out of office. "And I'd like to go down there and kick him out myself," he'd add fiercely. This was especially the case in President Wilson's two terms. There was something about Woodrow Wilson that made Father boil.

His dentist had made a bridge for him, at this time, to replace a lost tooth in front. Father soon took it back, "What's wrong, Mr. Day?" Dr. Wyant said. "Is the occlusion imperfect?"

"Why, your thing won't stay in; that's what's wrong with it," Father replied.

Dr. Wyant was puzzled. "You mean that the denture seems to work loose when you are at table?"

"No," said Father, "it stays in when I eat, and it usually stays in when I talk, but when I read my paper in the morning, and say what I think of that man Wilson, your thing pops right out."

So life wasn't boring in his old age to Father. He read more books then, too; particularly books about past and current political clashes. In these he always took sides. When his side won, he wanted their victory to be decisive; but if the other side won, they needn't hope to inflict a decisive defeat. The harder they pressed Father, the angrier and more determined he got; the more bloodthirsty, I was about to say, but he was always that, win or lose. This made reading an active and exciting way of spending his time.

He didn't care much for detective stories. The people in them were flashy. He no more wished to read about rascals than he did about saints. When he read fiction, he went back to Dickens or Dumas or Thackeray. In his forties he often bought paper-bound books on the train—W. Clark Russell's sea tales, or novels by a new man, R. L. Stevenson, which were then coming out. Some cost fifty cents, some twenty-five. And he always liked books about horses, provided they weren't sentimental. But problem novels, especially Mrs. Humphry Ward's, seemed to him bosh, also any books with triangles in them, or "men like that fellow Hamlet." Father preferred to read about people who knew their own minds.

He liked English history, but chiefly of the days before Cromwell. From about 1630 on, it was American Colonial times that he turned to, as though some ancestral self in him was retracing its steps.

One day Mother was persuaded, by a beautifully dressed woman book-agent, to buy on installment a set of *Memoirs of the French Court*. She never read them—she hated the hard cynical tone of that period, and "those wicked women who robbed the poor queens of their silly old husbands." And she wailed with remorse and despair when each installment fell due. A package of two volumes, at ten dollars apiece, was delivered each month. "Oh dear!" she would cry, as she hunted through her bureau drawers and her purse, to get twenty dollars together without using the Altar Society's money (which could never even be touched, it was so sacred, and yet was always sitting there, staring at her). "Those dreadful French creatures, they come so often I just can't stand it. I *did* hope there wouldn't be any *this* month. Why, if they are going to keep on coming like this I don't know what I shall do!"

She had been ashamed to tell Father about them. She hid the books from him. But when paying twenty a month became too harassing, as it very soon did, she burst in on him one day and said she had been buying him a present which she hoped he'd appreciate; and she dumped all she had of the French Court on his library table.

Father was startled. He put on his glasses suspiciously and said: "What the devil's all this?"

"Oh, *Clare,*" Mother said, impatiently pushing him, "don't be so *stupid*. It's the French Court, I tell you. It's a present for you."

"I don't want it," said Father.

"Yes you do too!" Mother shrieked. "You haven't even looked at it. It cost me enough, I can tell you. It's a very nice present."

She hurried back upstairs before he could refuse it again, leaving him wondering what she was up to.

The following month he found out. Two more volumes arrived, and she told him there was twenty dollars to pay on them. Father promptly exploded.

"But the messenger's waiting in the hall!" Mother cried.

"He can go and wait in hell!" Father shouted. "I hope he sizzles there, too."

"Oh Clare, he can hear you," Mother begged him. "Please, Clare. Do behave." And after the battle was over, Father was out twenty dollars.

"I thought you said those books were a present," he said to her, later.

"But not *all* of them, Clare," Mother said reproachfully, as though he was being too greedy. "The ones that I gave you were a present, but of course you must pay for the others."

Father bitterly warned her never to do such a fool thing again, and set to work to try to get his money's worth out of the French Court. He toiled through its oily intrigues as long as he could stand it, but he had to give up in disgust. He put away the kings, queens, and courtesans in an orderly row, with a yawn. They were nothing but a damned pack of foreigners. His ancestral self wasn't there.

One point I've left out is that each volume had the owner's monogram on it. This had made the set seem quite de luxe when the agent hypnotized Mother. But even then Mother had been doubtful about the French Court; she hadn't felt sure they were nice, though she had hoped for the best, and she thought it would be safer not to have her own monogram on them. So she had had the agent use Father's. This afterward seemed to prove she really had meant them to be a gift from the start. Father didn't believe it for a moment. Yet there was the evidence.

"I can't make Vinnie out," I heard him mutter, staring hard at the monogram.

They had been married for almost fifty years.

CHAPTER 30

FATHER PLANS TO GET OUT

ONE EVENING when Father and Mother and I were in the library talking, a trained nurse came in to take Mother's blood pressure, as the doctor had ordered. This was a new thing in Mother's life. It alarmed her. She turned—as she always did when she was in any trouble—to Father.

"Clare," she said urgently to him, "you must have yours taken too."

Father scowled at the nurse. Blood pressure was something which he had been hearing more about than he liked. He had just passed his seventieth birthday, many of his old friends had died, and when he and a few other survivors met at the funerals that came often now, Father had seen some of them shaking their heads and whispering things about "blood pressure." What angered Father about it was that it seemed able to kill healthy men—men who he had felt sure would last for the next twenty years. Like himself. He'd talk at the club with one of them in the evening, after a few games of billiards, and the next week he'd pick up the paper and see that that man had died.

Father said he wouldn't mind if people died only once in a while, as they used to. He said we all had to die, he supposed. But he didn't know what the matter was nowadays. Somebody died every month. And it never was a wizened old walnut, like John Elderkin, it was always some sound, healthy man. No excuse for it. When he asked his friends at the club to explain it, he never got a clear answer. All they could talk of down there was blood pressure.

He said he was beginning to hate all these funerals. They were getting to be disturbing and unpleasant things to attend. He told General Anderson he didn't see why they kept going to them. General Anderson frowned and said they had to. "If you don't go to other men's funerals," he told Father stiffly, "they won't go to yours." But Father said he didn't intend to die at all if he could help it, so they couldn't go to his anyway.

"When somebody dies, the people who loved them want to say goodbye," Mother said. "That's what I feel when I go to a funeral. You didn't use to mind going, Clare."

"Well, Vinnie," Father replied, "that was when I was younger. But what bothers me now is those parsons. Every time I go to a funeral they get out one of their books and read the part that says that the years of a man are threescore and ten. I know that I'm seventy but I'm as well as I ever was, hang it. I'm tired of hearing so much about this threescore and ten business."

The trained nurse stood there waiting. Father glared at her blood-pressure apparatus, and told her to take it away. "I don't know what it's all about," he said, "and I don't want to either. I won't have anything to do with this blood pressure."

"Everybody has blood pressure, Mr. Day," the nurse said.

"A lot of them have," Father replied, "but I haven't. I won't."

"If yours is all right," the nurse explained, "this little indicator will show it."

Mother said: "Please, Clare, let her take it, while the thing's right here in the house, and we don't have to pay a doctor to do it. It's costing enough for Miss Bassett—let's get our money's worth somehow."

"Oh well, pshaw," said Father, "if it will gratify your whim, go ahead."

Miss Bassett adjusted the strap on his arm. He sat there, red-faced and confident. She looked at the indicator. It recorded no special blood pressure.

Father laughed.

But Miss Bassett, examining the indicator again, saw that it hadn't worked; and when she readjusted it, the pressure was abnormally high.

"Pooh! What of it?" said Father; "all poppycock."

"No, Mr. Day, really," she said, "that condition is dangerous."

Father's face slightly stiffened. He stopped joking, rose with unwilling concern, walked away, grew quite angry, and said in a self-controlled tone that he didn't believe a word of it.

"You ought to take aconite, Mr. Day," the nurse told him.

"Pah! Never!" said Father.

His need seemed to be to forget it, put it out of his mind. I took some of the stable accounts out of my pocket, that I had been attending to for him. He usually hated to bother going over them with me. "May I ask you about these, Father?" I said.

He thankfully sat down at the desk and examined each item, and when we had finished he seemed to have sponged off his slate.

His arteries were beginning to get in poor shape, at that time. There were lots of things about his machinery that wouldn't have suited the doctors. I thought of how he hated to go to a dentist or oculist. I thought of how much food his digestion constantly had to put up with. But he seemed to make his machinery serve by expecting much of it. Perhaps that kept him hearty. He at least gave it no doubts to deal with, no doubts of itself.

Mother's habitual attitude was exactly the opposite. She read books on how to take care of herself, she tried different "health-foods," and the ominous warnings of advertisers frightened her dreadfully. But she came of a long-lived family, good hardy stock, and Father did too, and both of them lived to a ripe and far from languid old age.

Mother used to go to the cemetery in Woodlawn with her arms full of flowers, and lay the pretty things by some headstone, as a sign of remembrance. After a while she bought a cast-iron chair and left it out there, inside the square family plot, so that when it took her a long time to arrange her flowers she could sit down and rest. This was a convenience, but unluckily it was also a worry, because absent-minded visitors to neighboring graves began to borrow that chair. They dragged it off across the grass to sit and grieve in, and forgot to return it. Mother then had to hunt around for it and drag it back, which made her feel cross, and thus spoiled the mood she had come out in. She didn't like this a bit.

One Sunday when she herself was past seventy, and when Father in spite of his blood pressure and everything else was nearly eighty, she asked him if he wouldn't like to drive out with her to Woodlawn. She hadn't any flowers to take, but she had happened to think of that chair, though she didn't say so to Father. She merely said that it was a beautiful day and that it would do him good to go out.

Father refused. Positively. He winked robustly at me and said to Mother, "I'll be going there soon enough, damn it."

Mother said that he ought to come because one of the headstones had settled and she wanted him to tell her whether he didn't think it needed attention.

Father asked whose headstone it was, and when Mother told him he said: "I don't care how much it's settled. I don't want to be buried with any of that infernal crowd anyhow."

Mother of course knew how he felt about some of the family, but she said that he wouldn't mind such things when it was all over.

Father said yes he would. He became so incensed, thinking of it, that he declared he was going to buy a new plot in the cemetery, a plot all for himself. "And I'll buy one on a corner," he added triumphantly, "where I can get out!"

Mother looked at him, startled but admiring, and whispered to me, "I almost believe he could do it."